AF328611

Ashley Jackson: *The Yorkshire Artist*

Ashley Jackson: *The Yorkshire Artist*

A Lifetime of Inspiration Captured in Watercolour

Ashley Jackson

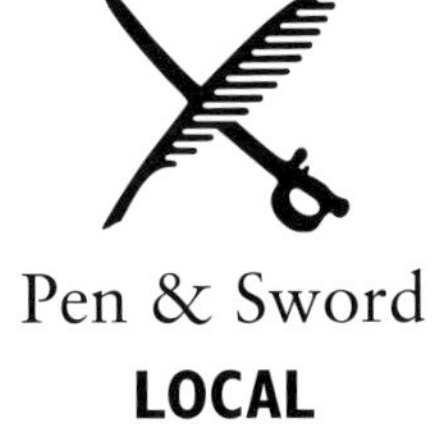

Pen & Sword
LOCAL

First published in Great Britain in 2017 by
Pen & Sword Local
an imprint of
Pen & Sword Books Ltd,
47 Church Street,
Barnsley,
South Yorkshire.
S70 2AS

A CIP record for this book is available from the British Library.

ISBN 978 1 47389 800 4

Printed and bound by Replika Pvt Ltd, India

Pen & Sword Books Ltd incorporates the Imprints of Pen & Sword Aviation, Pen & Sword Maritime, Pen & Sword Military, Wharncliffe Local History, Pen & Sword Select, Pen & Sword Military Classics and Leo Cooper.

For a complete list of Pen & Sword titles please contact
Pen & Sword Books Limited
47 Church Street, Barnsley, South Yorkshire, S70 2AS, England
E-mail: enquiries@pen-and-sword.co.uk
Website: www.pen-and-sword.co.uk

Contents

Foreword

Like most Yorkshire people I work and live in an urban area. Our industrial heritage is a source of great pride and I am immersed in projects to regenerate it. But where is the county's soul?

You must turn your eyes to the 'tops' – to the hills, to the valleys and moorlands that are never far away, even if you are based in a town or city. Poets and authors have distilled the essence of our landscapes – the Brontës spring to mind – but visual art offers an immediate and vivid way to capture Yorkshire's moods, from benign and beautiful to harsh and uncompromising.

To achieve this, you must be a poet with your paintbrush and you must have an abiding passion for Yorkshire. Ashley Jackson has these qualities in abundance.

His technique is unimpeachable, but his vision and unquenchable love for our landscapes, in all their temperamental glory, are the elements that make him Yorkshire's artist laureate.

The places he depicts are timeless and the same goes for his work. But this book makes that point far more effectively than any words of mine . . .

Professor Bob Cryan CBE DL FREng
Vice-Chancellor, University of Huddersfield

Dedication

To my daughter Claudia Berettoni, I wish to thank her for bringing together this unique collection of paintings and collaborating with me not just on this book but over the last fourteen years.

Preface

As you know, I truly believe that if Ashley were to be cut in half he would say Yorkshire through and through, such is his passion for the landscape that we call 'God's County' . . . important as his words are it really is for his paintings to speak for themselves. The raw passion and dramatic atmosphere of an incoming storm or the flashes of colour in a moorland fire, he is adept at emotionally connecting you with his imagery because it is truly a love affair and besides his wife there is nothing else that comes close. He may be alone on the moor but not in the emotional, isolated way that many would feel, when stood out in the open landscape without a soul in sight.

This book, his paintings and his project 'Framing the Landscape' will be his legacy. I know that I am biased, as I am his daughter but, putting family loyalties to one side, I sincerely believe his paintings, like a good bottle of wine, have gained more depth, tone and power through the years . . . not to say that he has rested, for the last fifty years he has honed his skills, becoming more at one with his mistress.

Claudia Berettoni

Introduction

The Yorkshire moors have always pulled at my inner soul from the young age of nine years old and now as my age moves as quickly as cat's eyes on the motorway, I can honestly say I have grown deeper in love with her. For she is a woman to me; with her soft and wild nature, the perfumed scent of heather blowing around you and her voice, the wind blowing in your face. How can you not paint her beauty when she enthrals you?

I have been sincerely fortunate for I have been in heaven for the last sixty years, whilst being able to bring up a family solely from my love of the Yorkshire moors captured within a watercolour through my hands, my passion and my eyes.

> *Years go by as fast as cat's eyes on a motorway.*
> *The art of living is to make use of what*
> *you've got and use it to the full.*
> *Most people don't know what they are*
> *living for, but once you have found out*
> *you have the jewel of life.*
> (Ashley Jackson, 1969)

This book contains paintings old and new from the last fifty-four years of my life, each holding a different chapter. I hope that you will read my love letters from Mother Nature and my soul with enjoyment.

It is not a book that needs to be read from start to finish but is one that can be picked up and put down, savouring each page as an individual chapter, immersing yourself in the landscape and perhaps bringing with it your own personal memories of a location you too might have visited.

Throughout my career I have tried to be the people's artist, wishing my paintings to be accessible and not requiring a dictionary or 'this way up' written behind it so that when exhibited curators know which way to hang them. I wish my paintings to speak for themselves.

Ashley Jackson

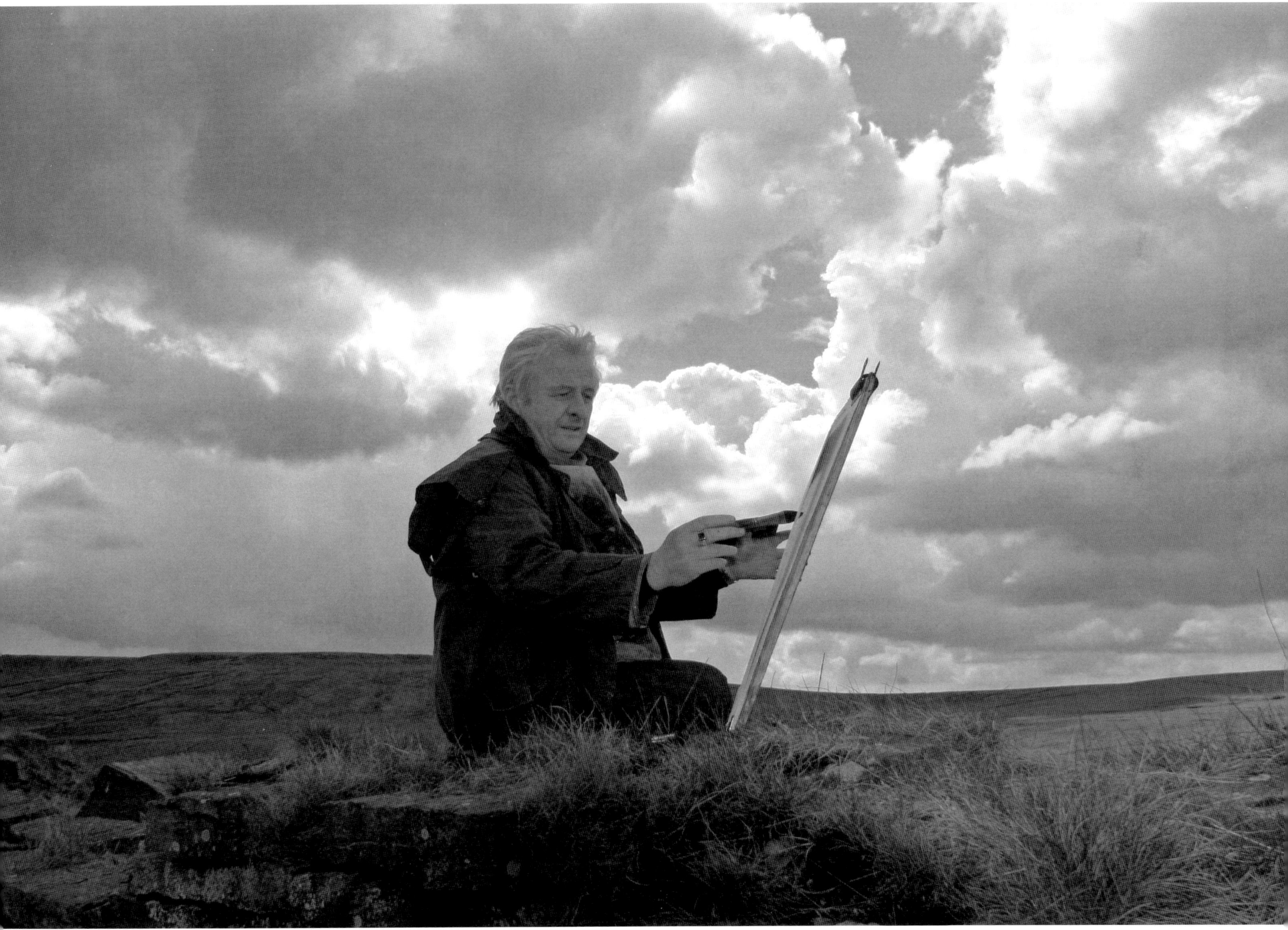

Autumn Solitude

Alone with my thoughts and mistress, the moor.

You are never truly alone on the moor, with the wind blowing through your hair, feeling the sun on your face, for your inner self is with you and your soul will talk to you in spirit.

The sun will burn you
The rain will wet you,
The wind will chill you,
But only people will make you cry
So paint what you feel and not
What will sell.
(Ashley Jackson, 1962)

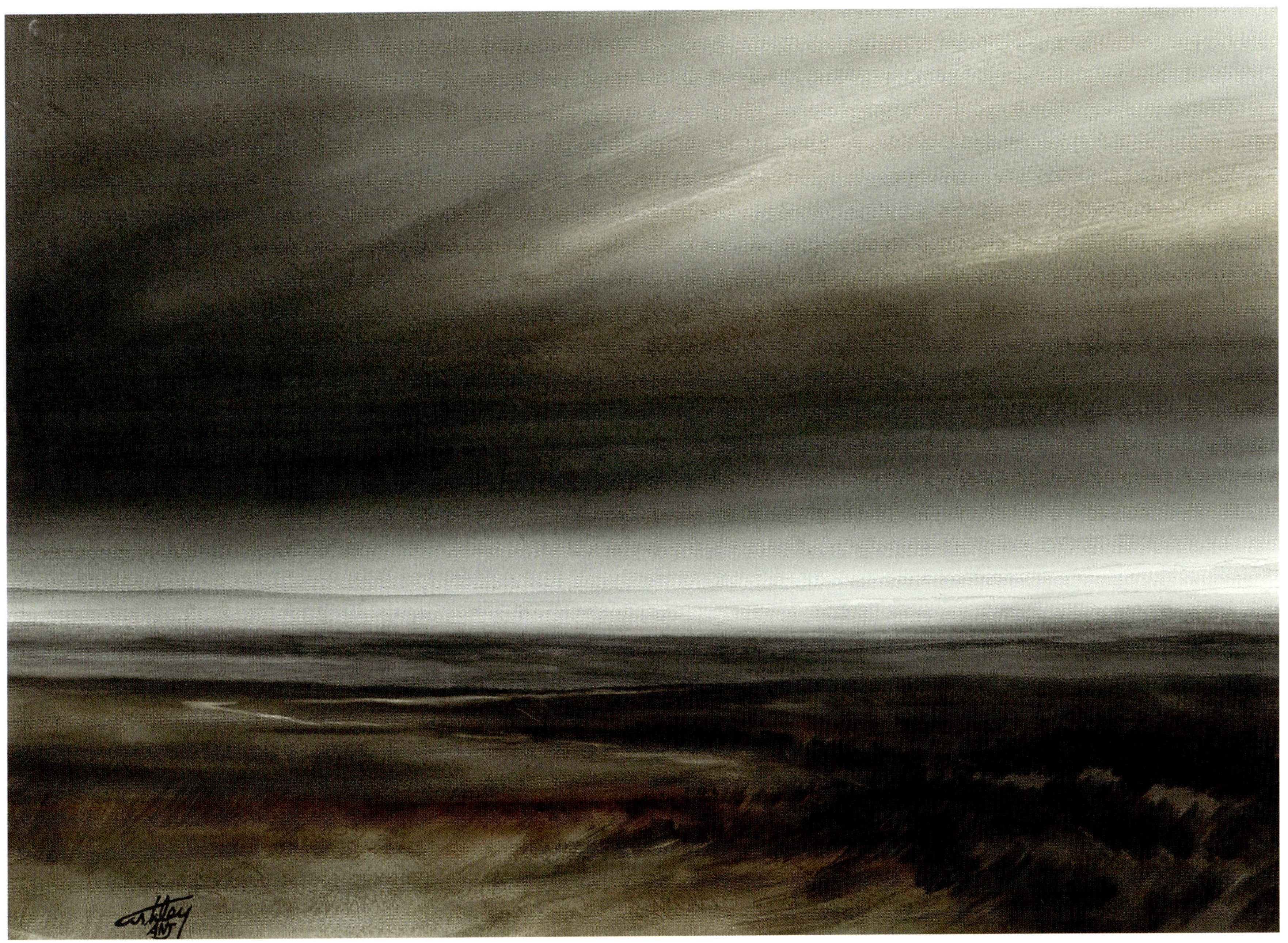

Earth to Earth, Life's Pathway

I have tried to capture a strong reminder of how small we are in the grand scheme of life. Mother Nature is as harsh as snow blizzards on an isolated moor, or as gentle as morning sunlight on the grass, but of all life's certainties, she will carry on without us.

I am still hungry and art is still the blood that courses through my veins, but if I died tomorrow I know that I have lived . . . (Ashley Jackson, 2010)

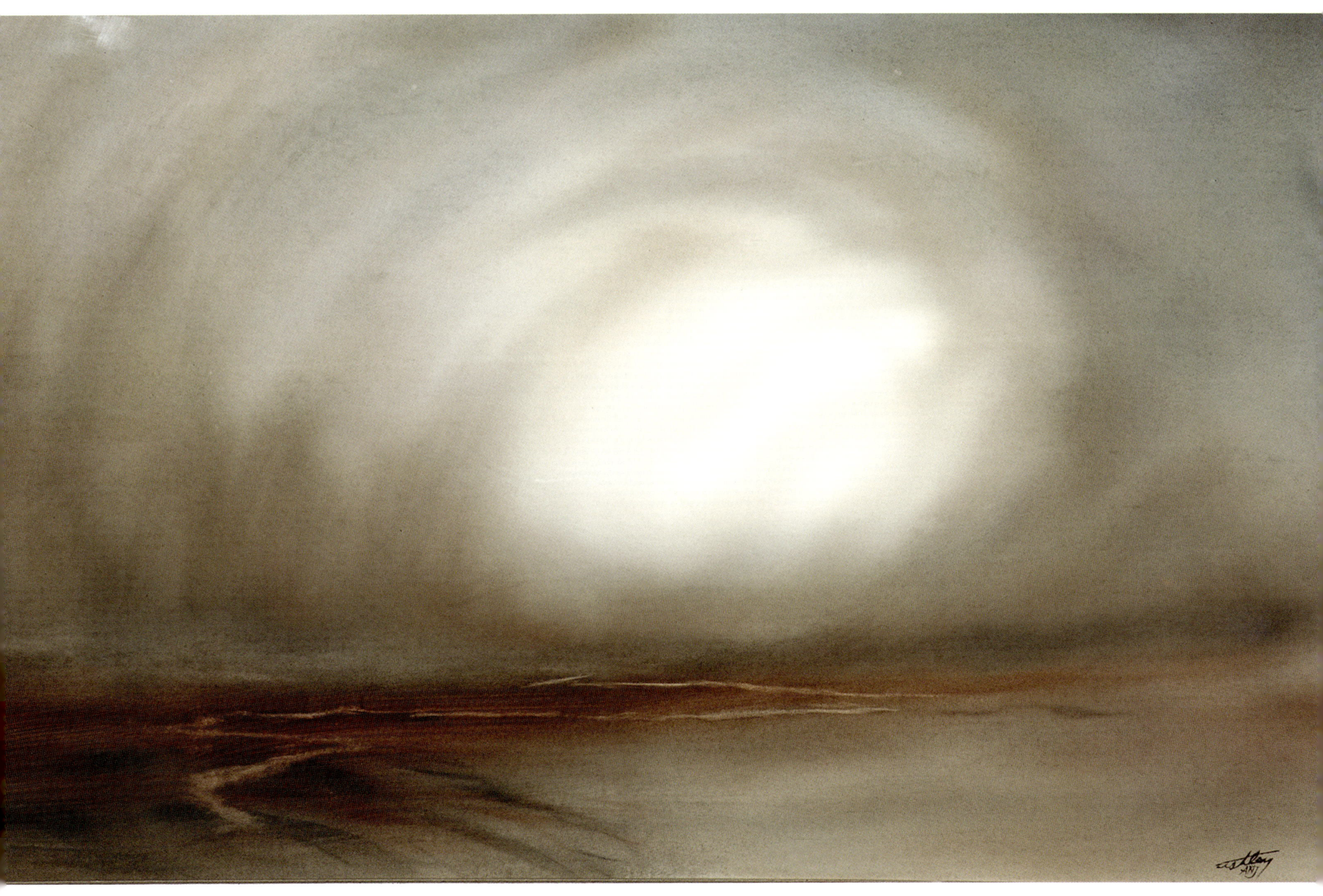

Fire on Saddleworth Moor

Although most fires are destructive, moorland fires, when started for the right reasons and not arson, are a rejuvenating process. From out of the ashes new growths seek the newly-created daylight. Previously smothered by old growth, the new is given the chance of life.

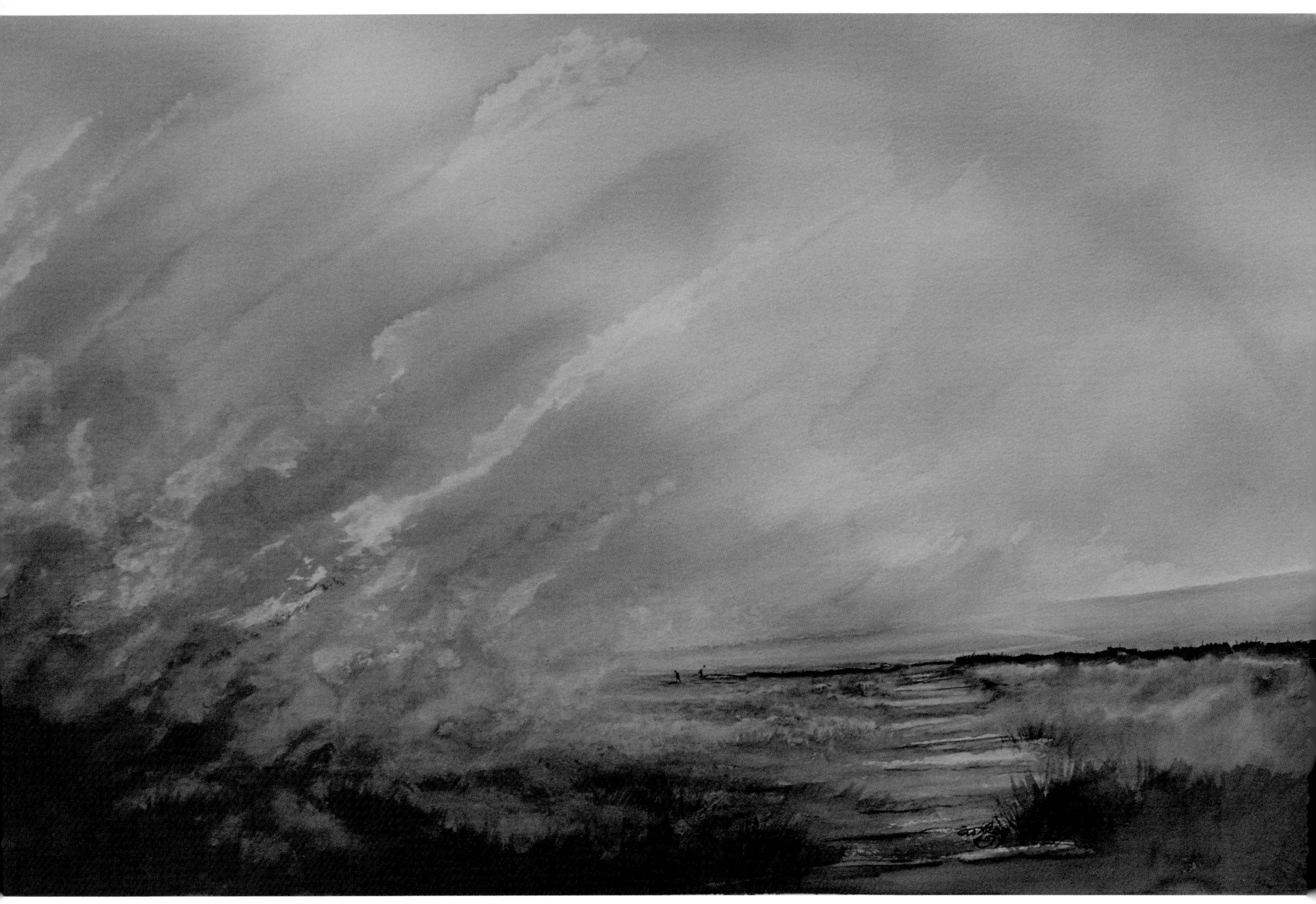

Ma, Look what they have done to my moor

I do believe that climate change is occurring all the time and will continue to occur when we have all passed on. The Earth is a new planet and is constantly changing. As I have been upon these moors for over fifty years I have only seen miniscule changes to the landscape. Global warming is taxation and scaremongering: man is destroying the world helped by 25 square feet of concrete below each turbine. What happens to this when the windmill is no longer productive, who will remove this from our landscape? This is money-making vandalism.

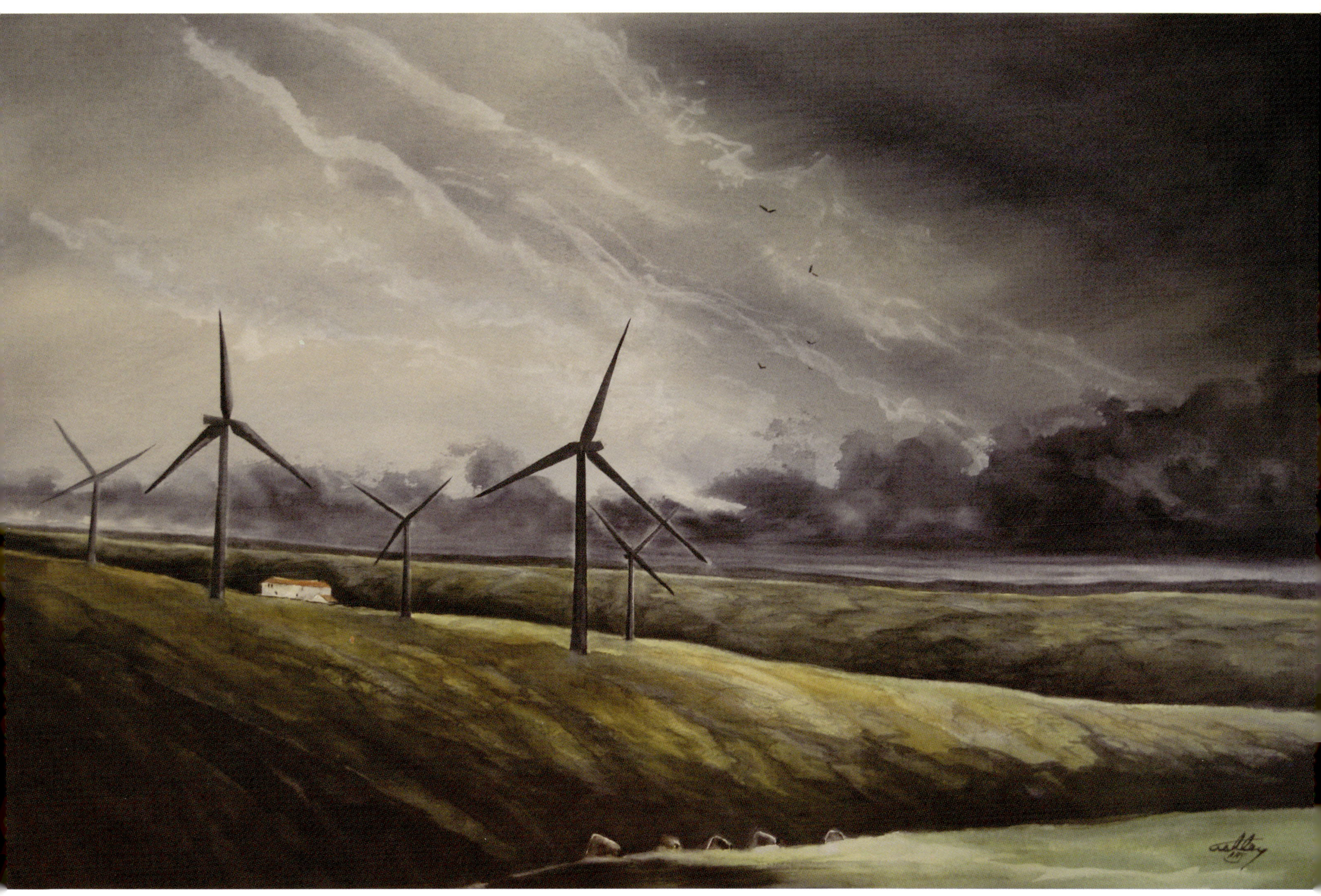

Clearing Mist

When painting *Clearing Mist* I could feel the 'Spirit of the Moor' descending on the landscape, with a glow of light one can't forget. The light within this painting is the white of the paper for I use no white paint . . . ever.

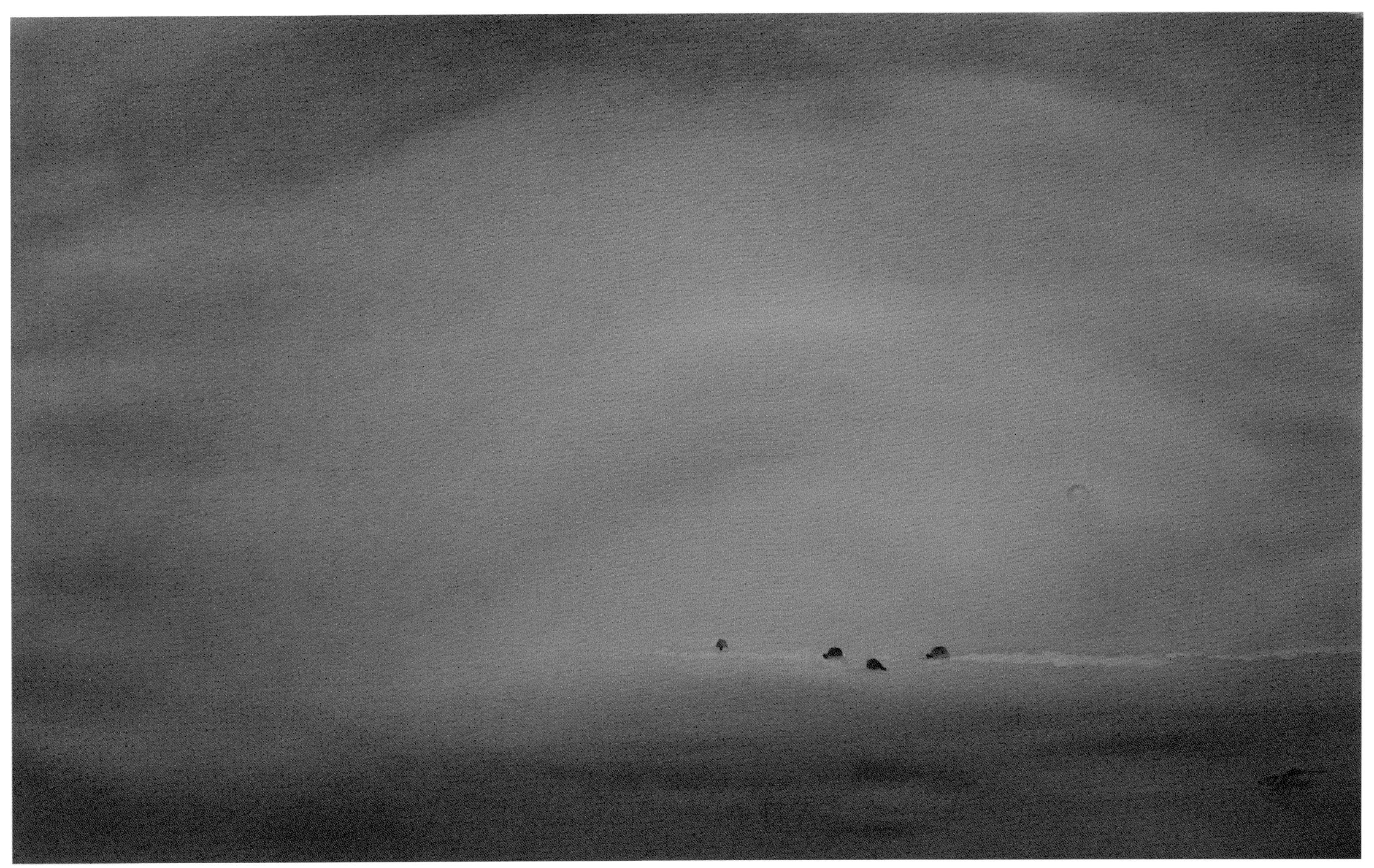

When All have Gone Home

The close of the day, when darkness descends and night rules the foreboding moors.

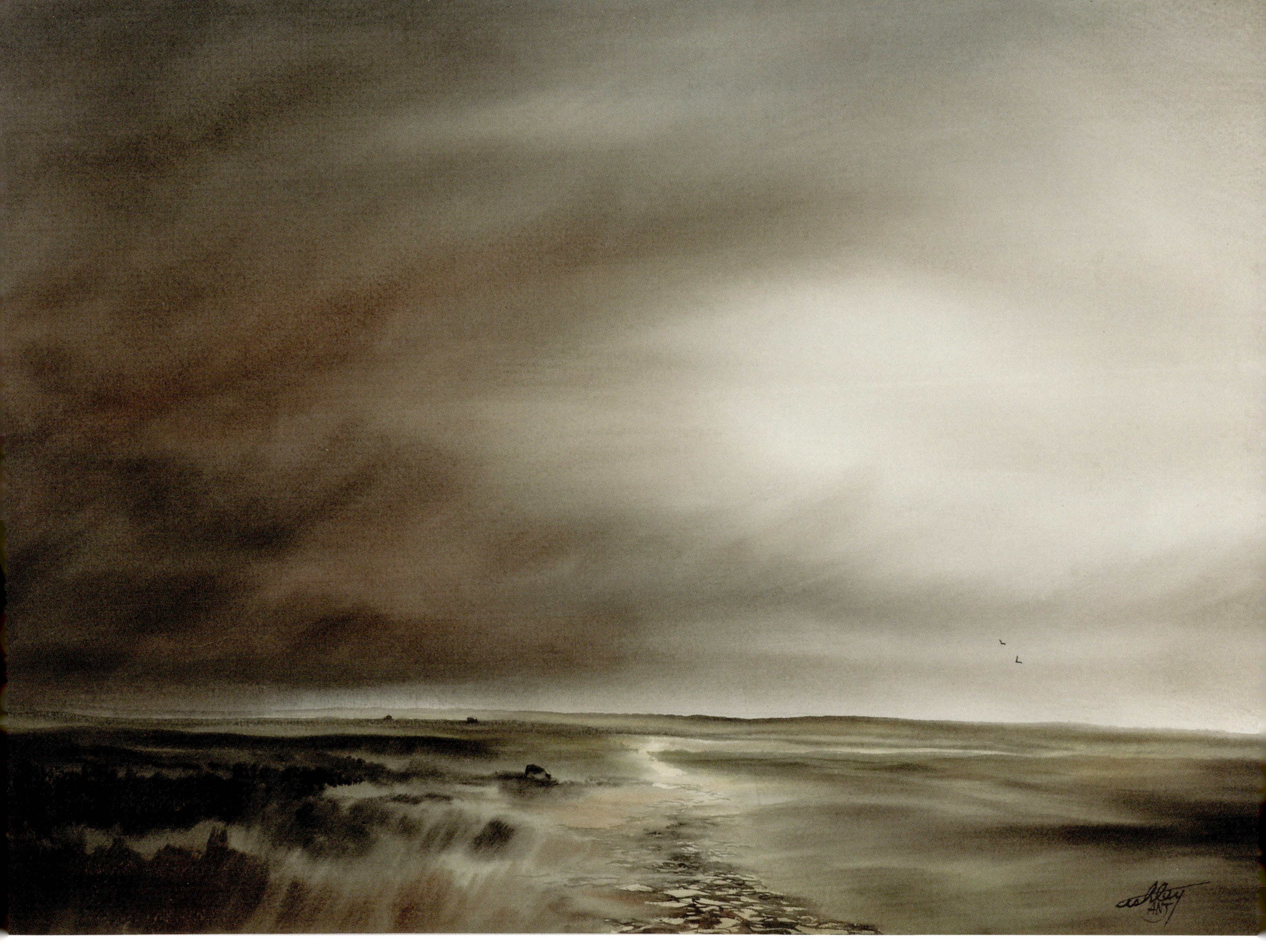

Low Cloud Lifting

When up here on my own, painting away from the madding crowd, I was overcome by a feeling that I could not truly explain; that the low cloud was swirling on the moor, giving me the feeling that God was present. I have tried to capture the mysteriousness of the event within this painting.

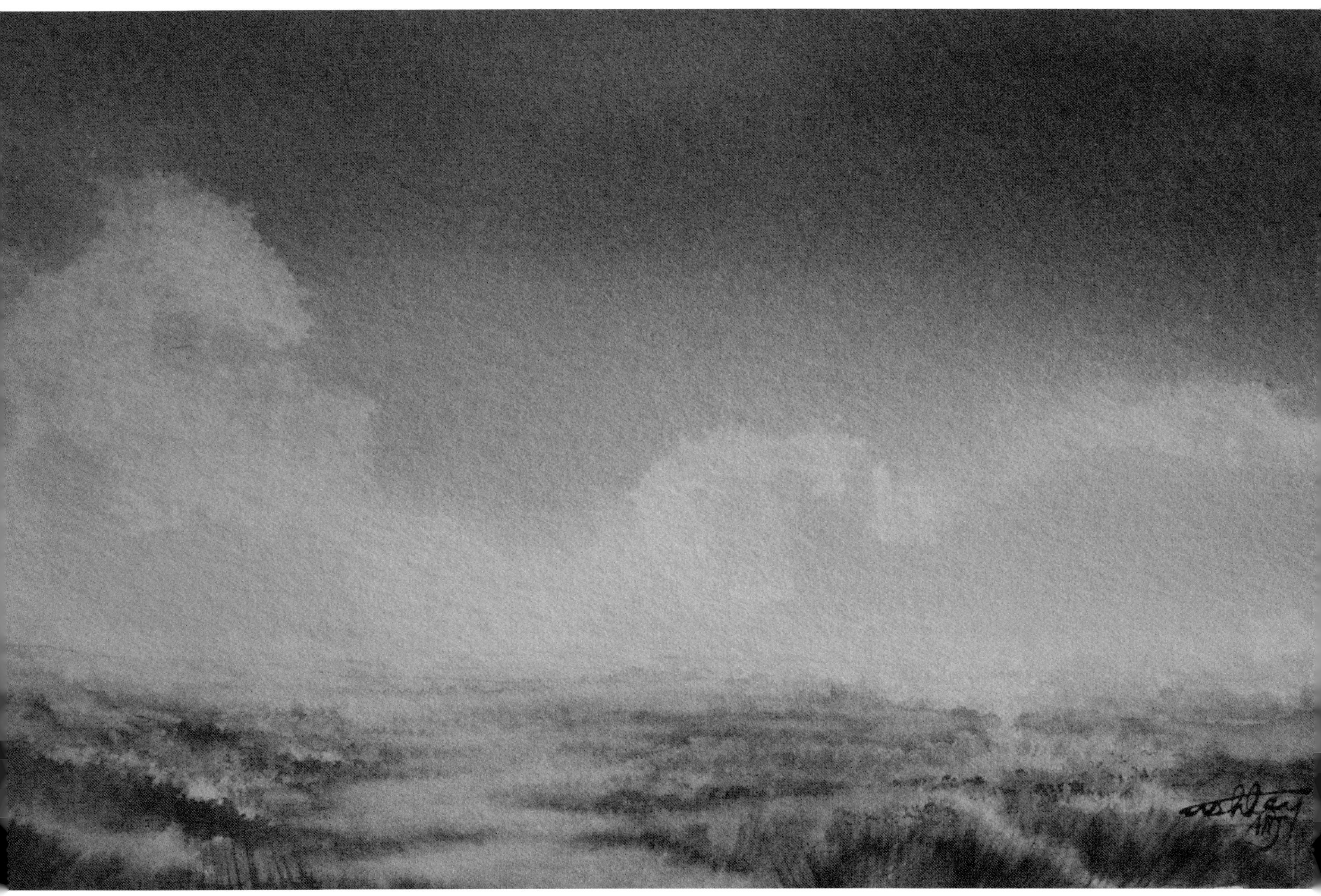

Power and the Passion

Turner is the master of all skies: I look for the light as Turner did and most of all I look for my mistress on the moor. Working in the, Great Cathedral, of the open air, I try to capture the echoes in the sky, looking through a tunnel to focus the eye moving within the painting. There are more than thirty washes of colour within this painting: it is only through my years of knowledge of which colours are transparent and those that are opaque that allows all the individual colours to be seen and not end as one muddy mess.

This was the central painting to the 'Power and the Passion' exhibition, a one-man show throughout all three galleries in The Mall Galleries, London, in celebration of my 70th year. It was my vision to showcase a small number of my largest works, often 5ft by 4ft in their mounted and framed size with a paintings-space of white wall left remaining between each. Yes, I know as a Yorkshireman I could have filled the walls with work, but I wished each of the limited number of paintings that I personally chose to be an invitation to view the Yorkshire landscape, to see Yorkshire through my eyes, heart and soul. The individual paintings were more important than the overall number on display, for each one was to speak to the person standing in front of it, to imprint a memory and emotion. Benches were provided for such personal reflection. The wildlife artist David Shepherd was most generous on his visit to the exhibition, commenting of my paintings that, 'No one could paint watercolours to the size and depth as Ashley Jackson'.

The exhibition returned to Yorkshire to Temple Newsam House, Leeds, in time to celebrate my birthday on 22 October 2010.

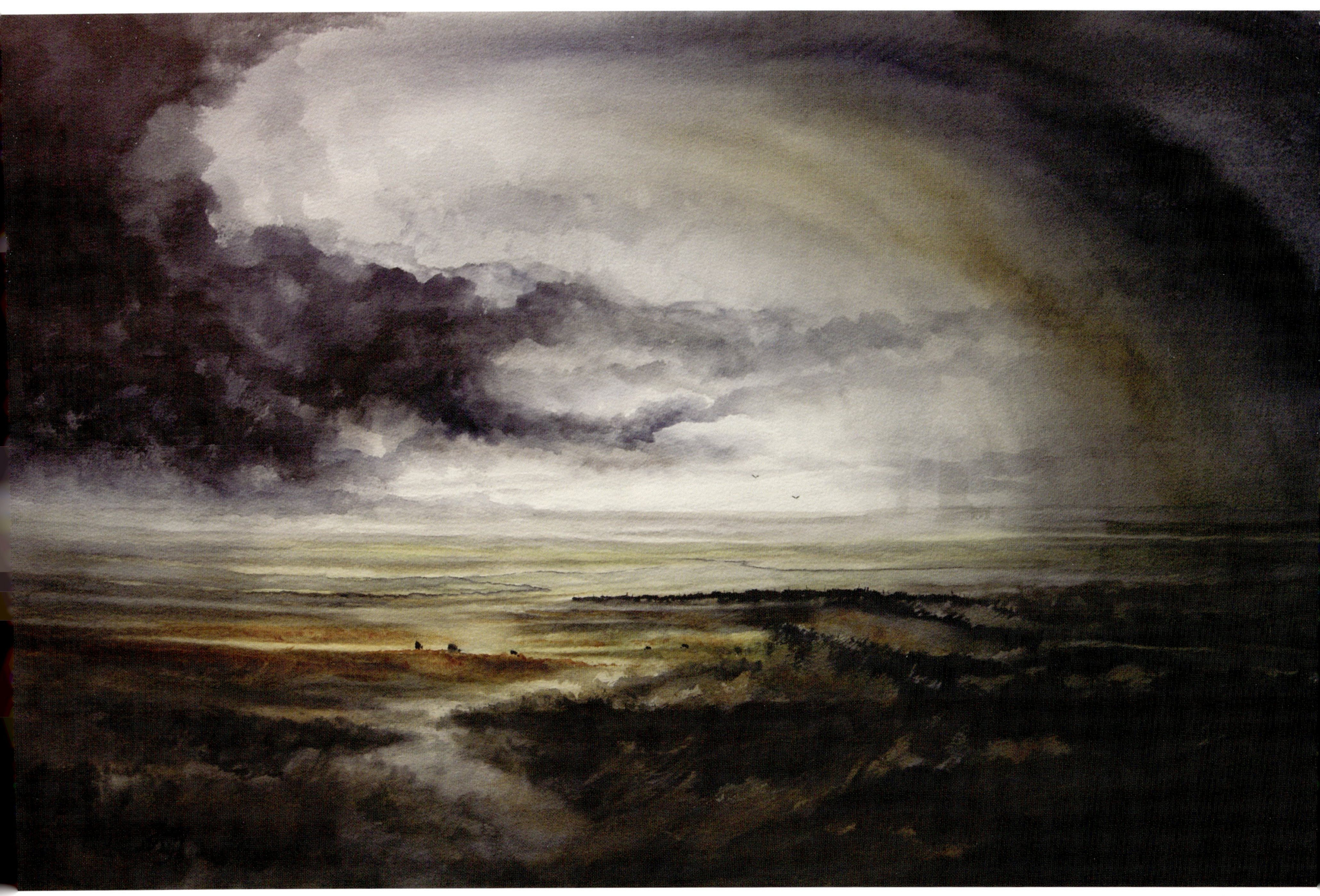

When the Curtain Comes Down

I seem morbid, but I have always had my inner self, in other words my soul.

I have been fortunate to have this passion and light in life, this painting reminds me of my finale – when the curtain comes down. On this day, you could not only visibly see the darkness descend but with it came a cold dampness that chilled you through to the bone.

Time is for ever
There is no death, only
a change of place:
to see and feel the moor
see light and feel and
smell the bracken
let alone paint it
is indeed an honour.
(Ashley Jackson, 1966)

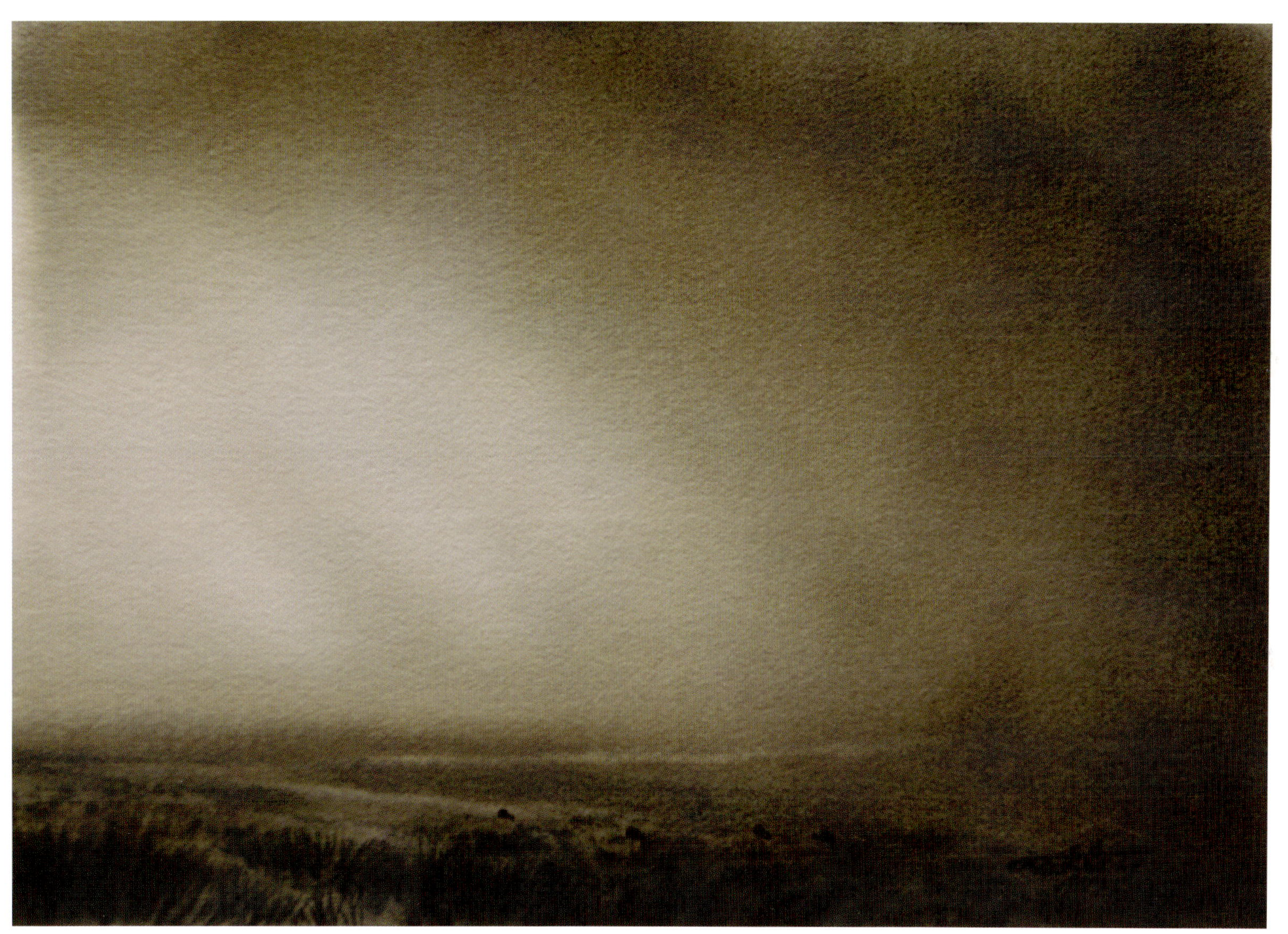

Chasing Light

As a boy I used to play a game where I would sit on the wall and watch the shadow of the clouds racing across the landscape, chasing the contours. I always felt that the shadows were chasing the light. For an artist, light is the essence of your painting, for without it you have no shape or colour. I still chase that light . . .

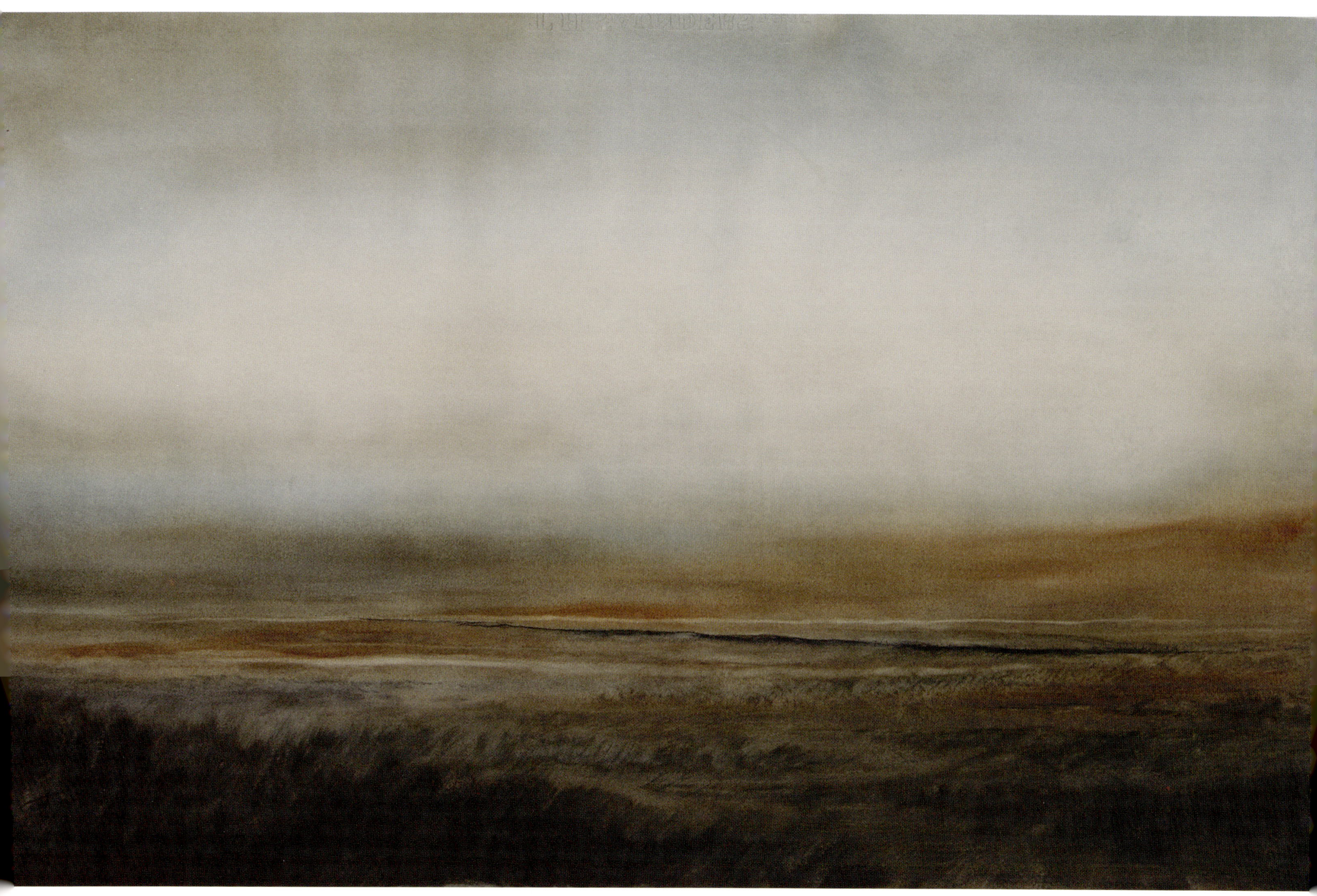

Passing Storms

As an artist I have been privileged to view the moors with an honest clarity: the drama of the sky with an approaching storm, the crispness of fresh-fallen snow underfoot or the damp chill of drizzling rain. The landscape is more than a passing view from a car window – it is our heritage, culture and, more personally, it forms part of our thoughts and feelings. The moving tunnel of light reminds us that as bad as they may seem all storms will pass and, like the farmhouse on the hillside, we too will weather the storm.

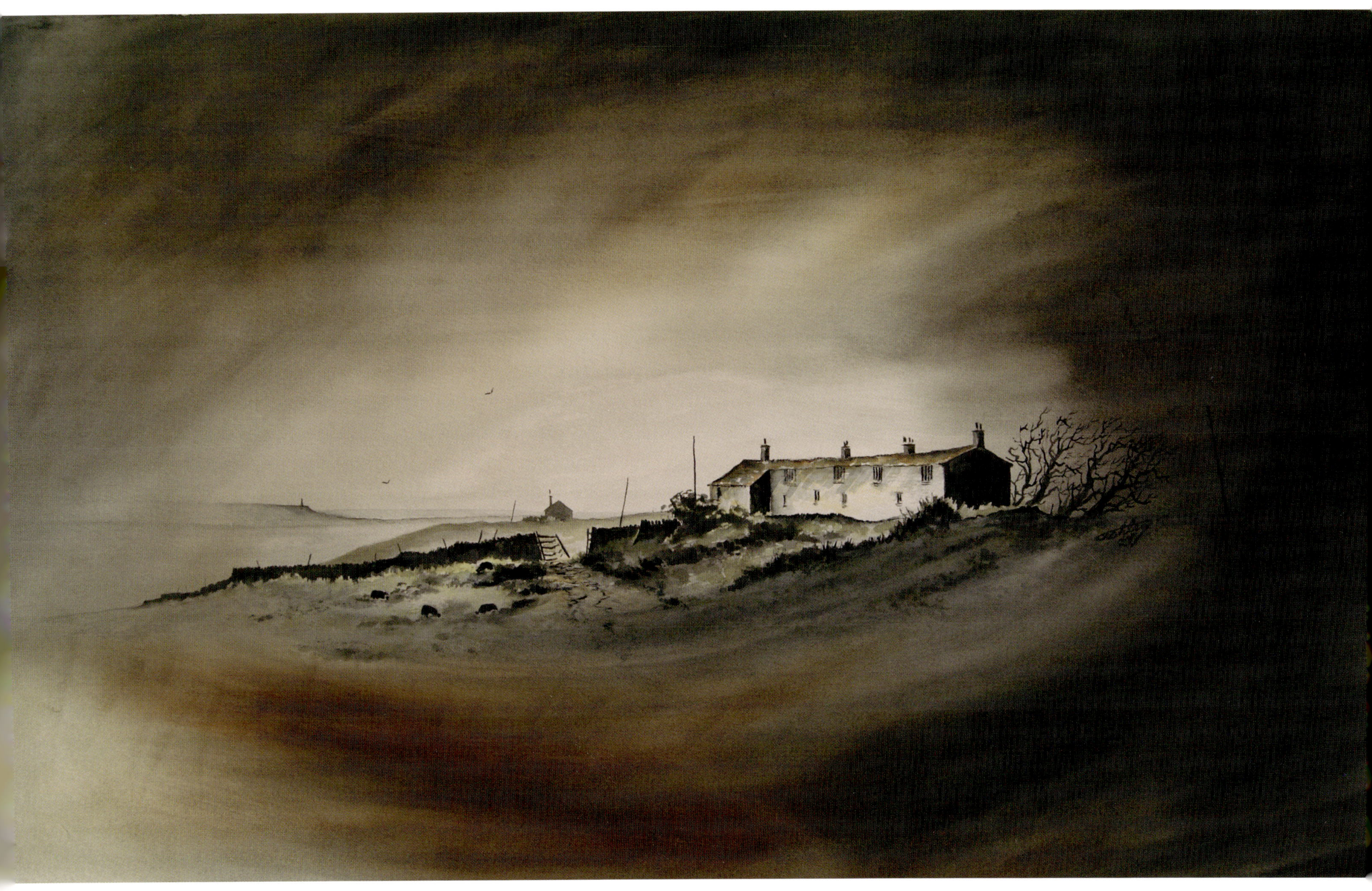

This is God's County

I have never wanted to be the genius of the chocolate box; I have tried for the last fifty years to capture Yorkshire in its entirety. Many will perhaps be surprised to see the warmth of colour and brightness within this painting, for I am perhaps known more for capturing the dark dramatic skies and storm clouds, but for me the challenge was in the natural reflection of the sky and the landscape.

The title is self explanatory: as a Yorkshireman absorbed in this lifelong love affair with the landscape of Yorkshire, I truly believe that it is God's County.

Give me the arts, for art is beauty.
Beauty is also in a woman.
But when I stand upon these moors,
I see beauty that never dies.
But woman's beauty fades with time.
And equal to beauty is companionship,
Which woman has.
Funny with both these gifts one cannot
touch them.
Which is beauty in itself.
(Ashley Jackson 1967)

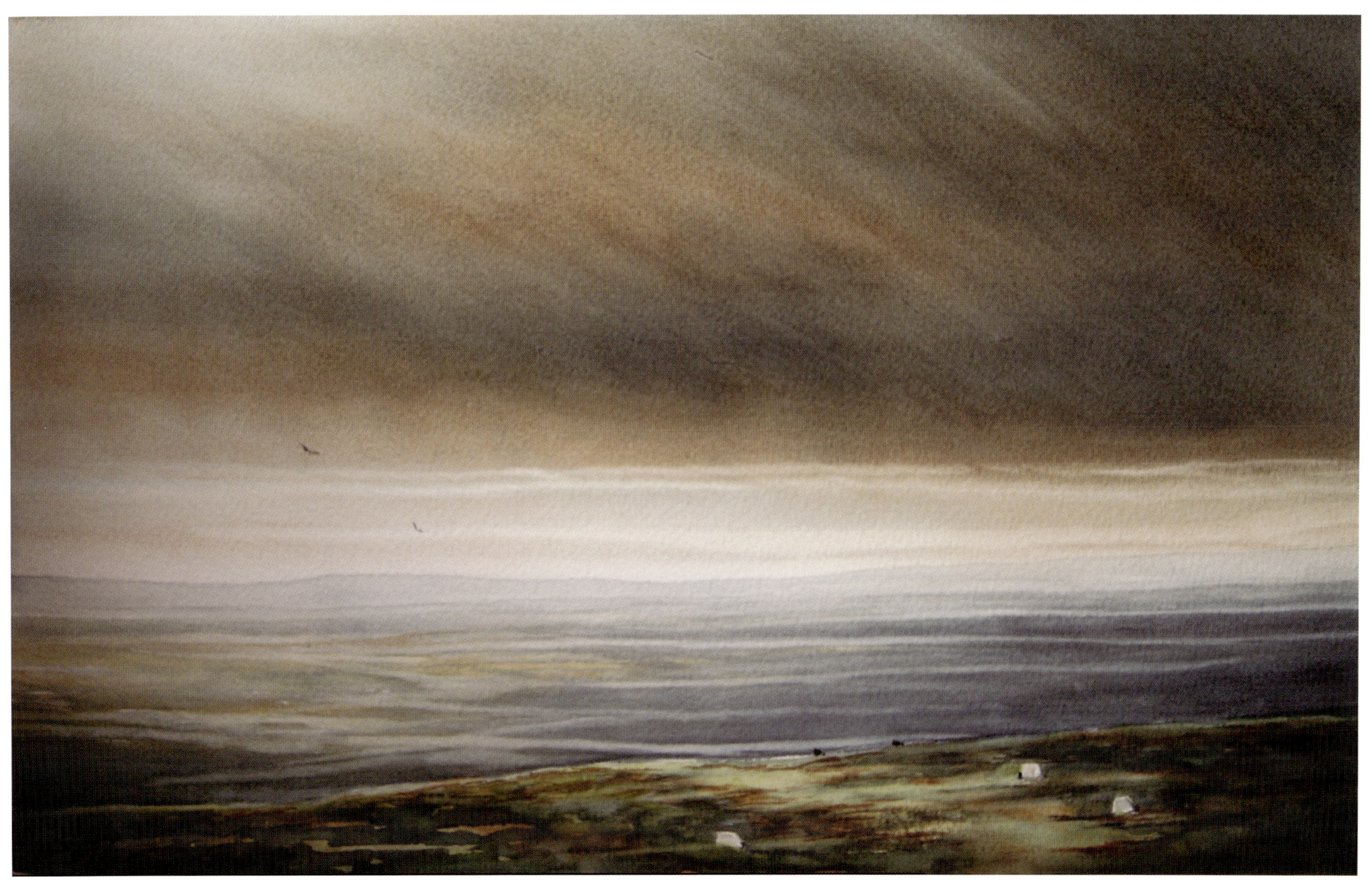

Moving Light – Gordale Scar

Moving Light captures the sun's glow as it passes along the hillside at Gordale Scar, North Yorkshire, creating luminous highlights in the grass and hedge.

I have visited Gordale Scar many times in my life and I think I could count on one hand the number of days that have been dry . . . One of my last visits was following in the footsteps of Turner, filming for Calendar ITV: the rain removed the layers of watercolour paint as quickly as I was putting the washes on.

Speaking to a group of adults and children that had been camping nearby, a golden moment was when one of the young lads said:'I know you, I pass your gallery every day, you're Sam's grandpa aren't you?' All of which was captured on the sound equipment, much to the amusement of the Calendar team. It goes to show the world is always much smaller than you think: they had come camping to Gordale Scar with their parents from Holmfirth.

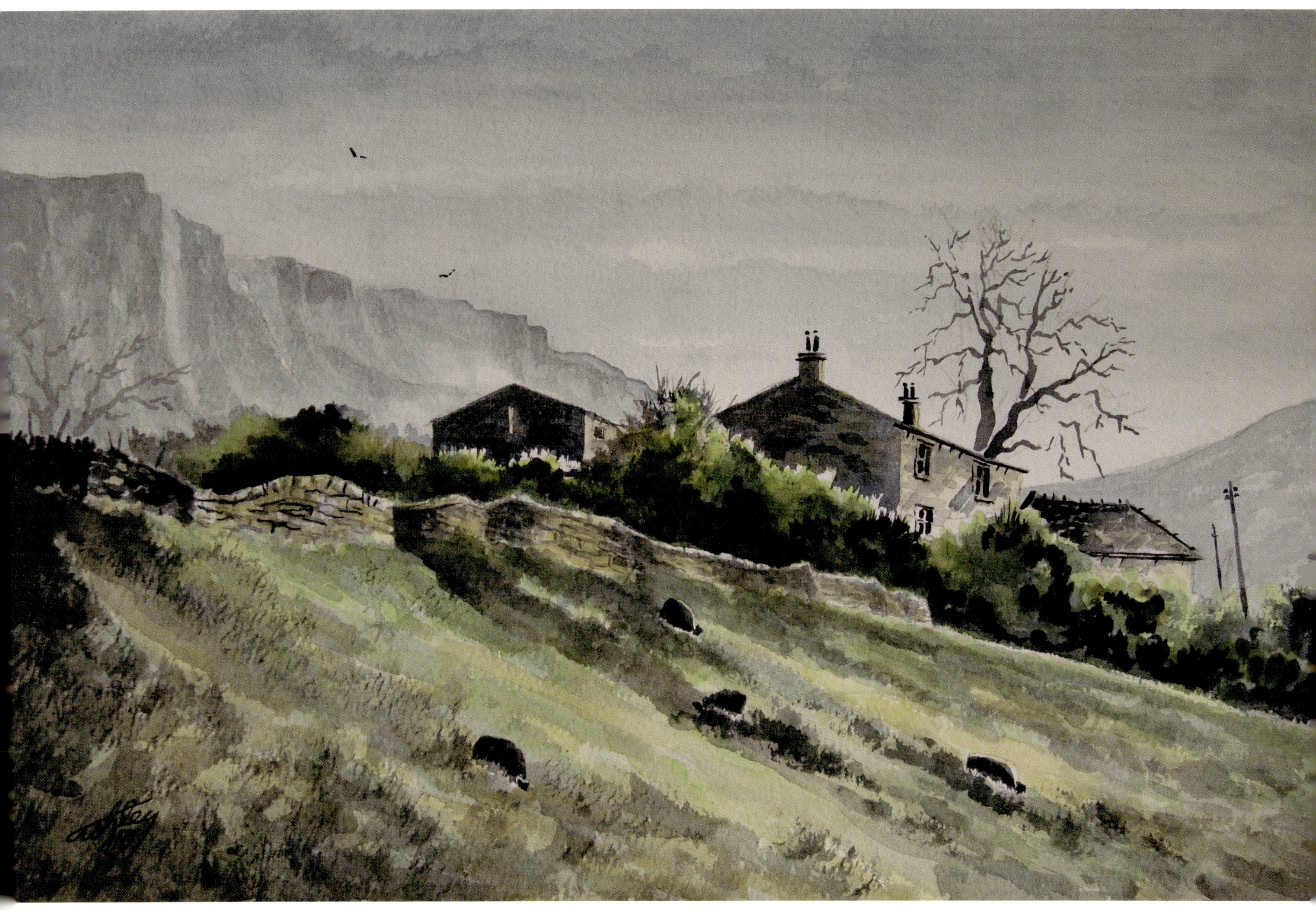

Moving Light – Gordale Scar   37

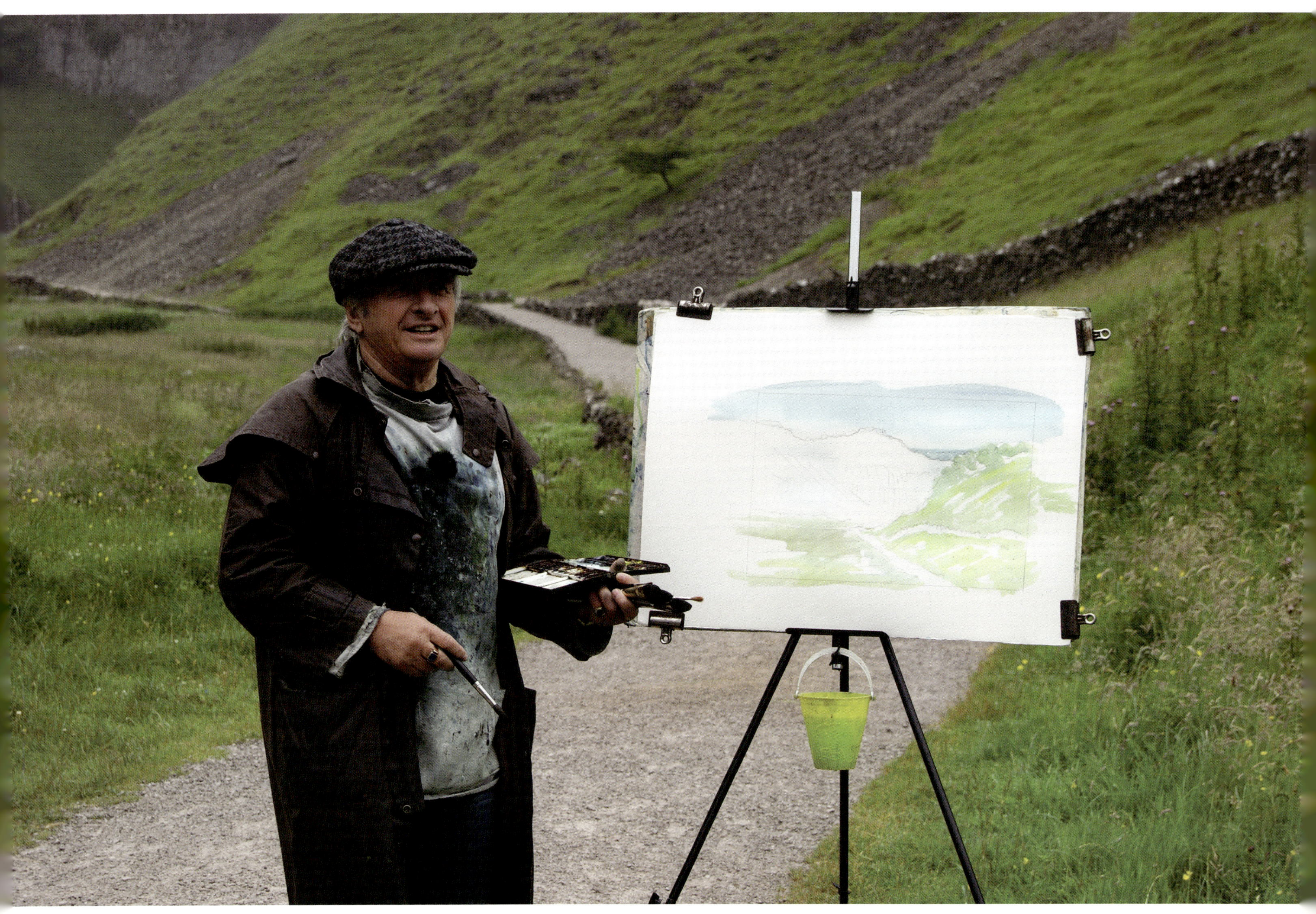

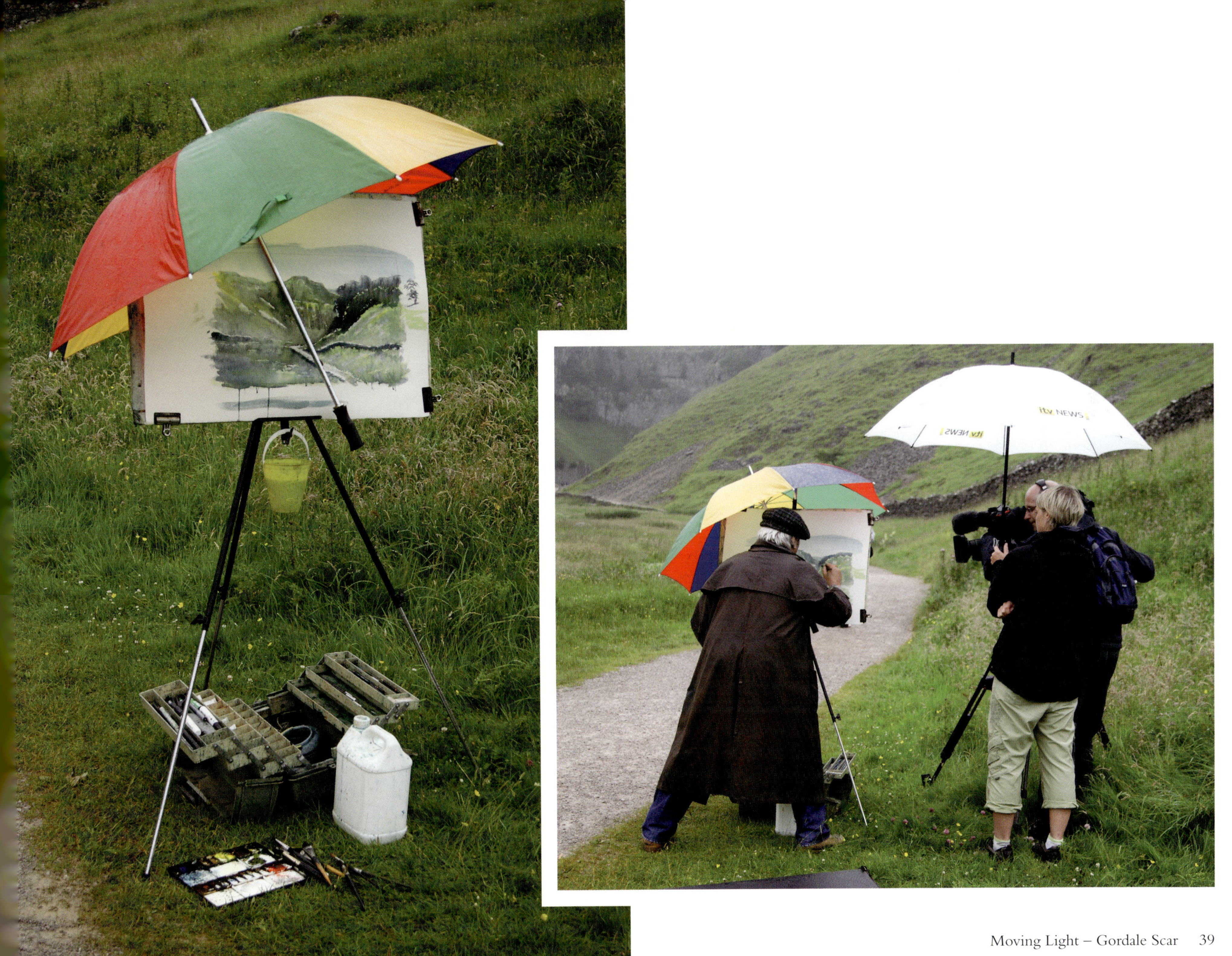

Solace from the Storm – Hilltop farm, Meltham

The quiet of the winter storm having past is replaced with birdsong, fresh shoots and life returns to normal. The inhabitants of the farmhouse are as hardy as the sheep, finding a way to survive against all that nature throws at them. It reminds us that for all our differences, we are all the same.

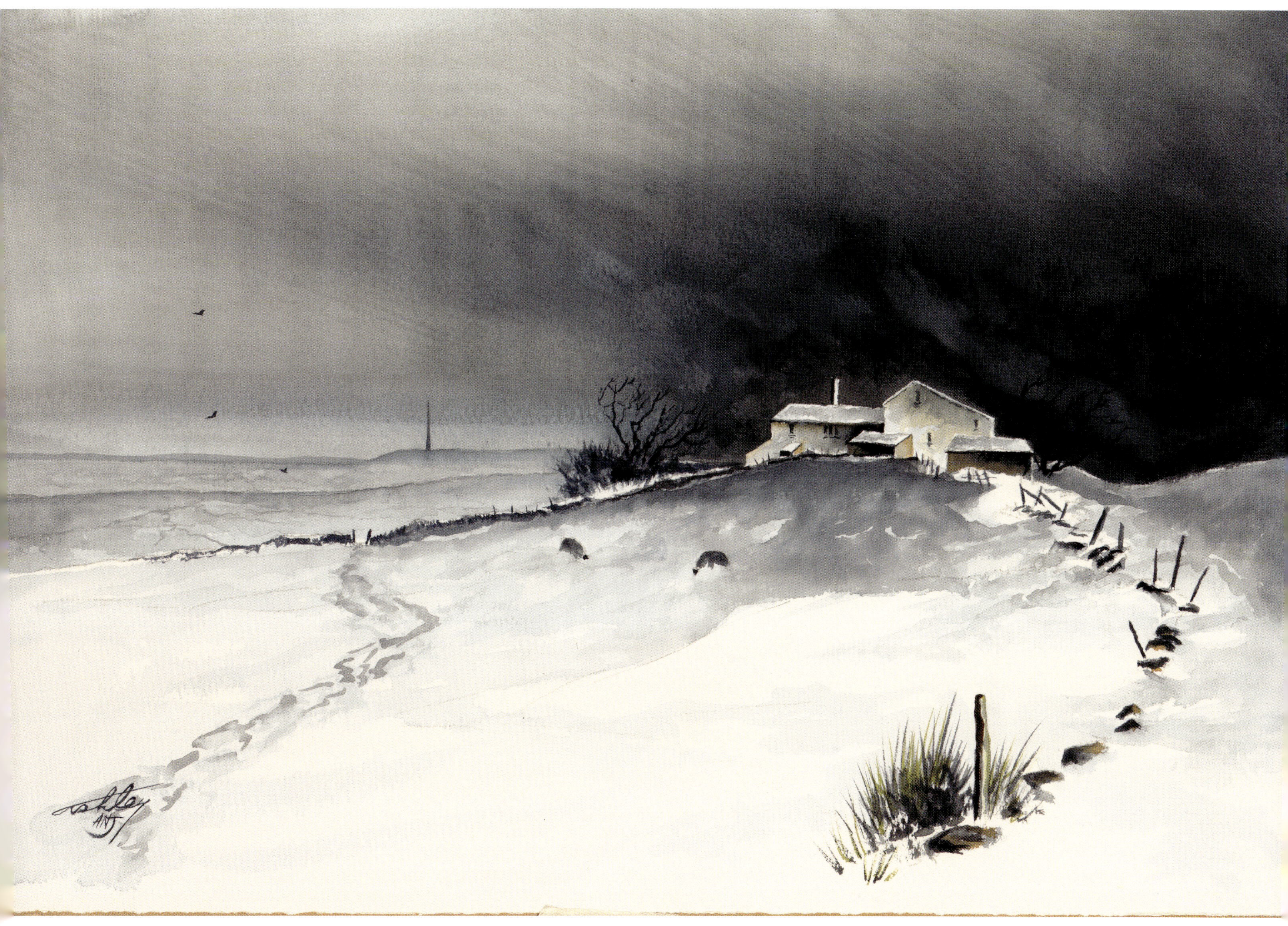

Moment of Clarity – Penyghent in the distance

Do we not all seek that moment of clarity, like an epiphany when suddenly a weight is physically or mentally lifted . . . we might not even have known we were carrying an extra load but the open moorland seems to spiritually seep into every pore, making us lighter and the world a little easier to see.

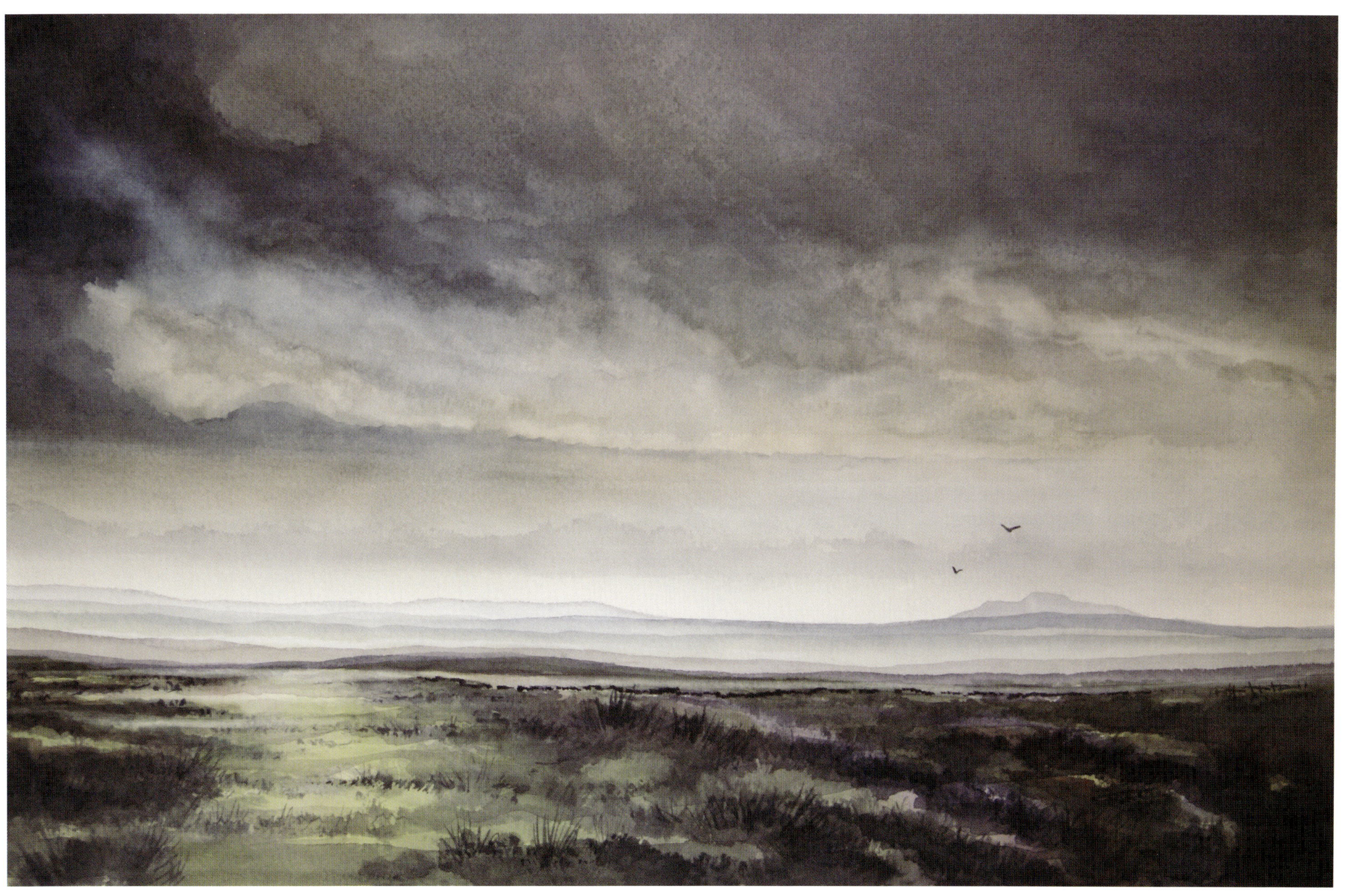

Spring on its Way – Widdup Moor

Although there is a dramatic storm breaking in the skies above, within the dark atmospheric clouds you can see a glimmer of warmth, a sign that winter is about to break and be replaced by the new light of spring.

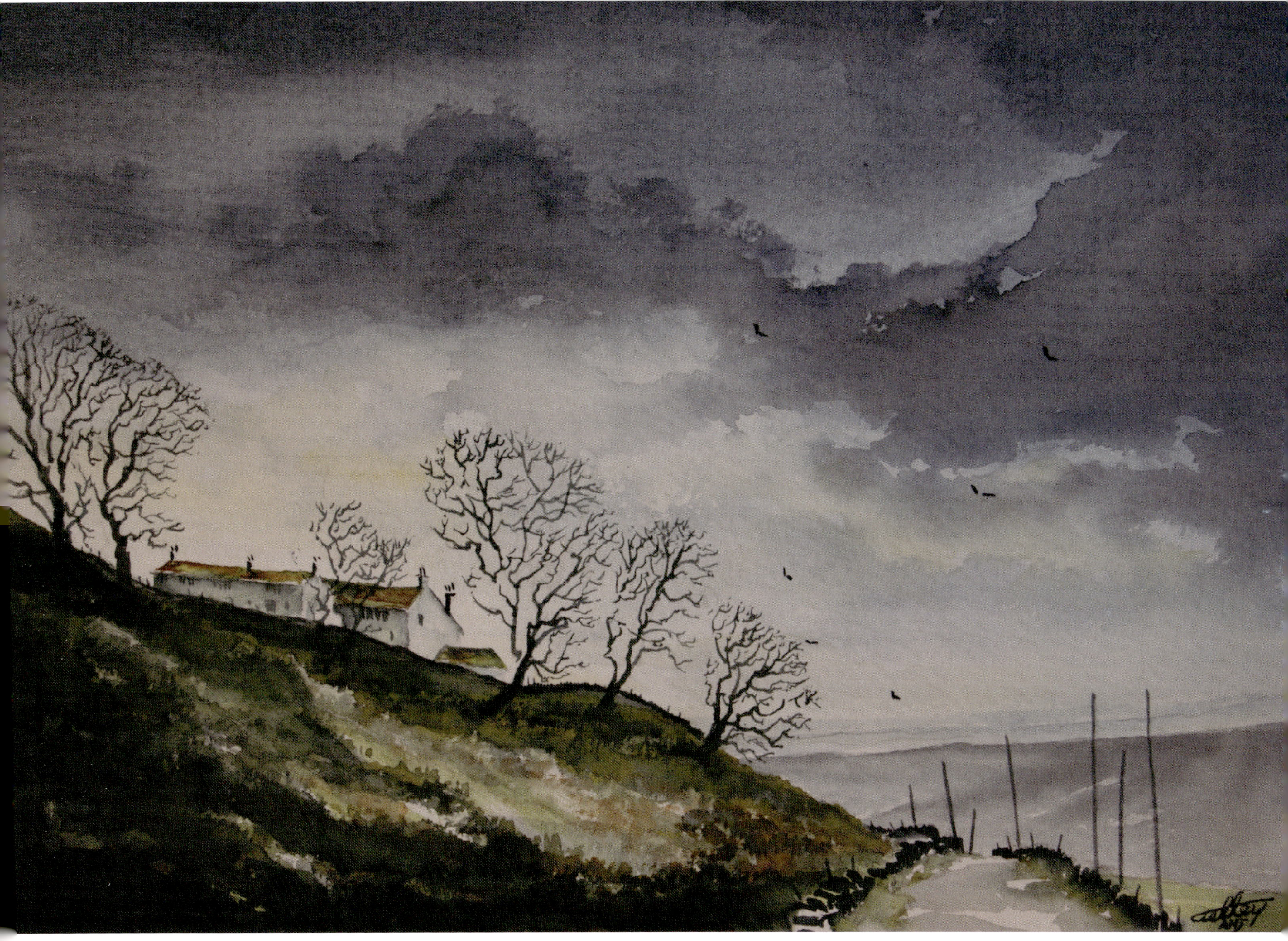

Staithes

Staithes is a village suspended in time. Once one of the largest fishing villages on the north-east coast, it is now familiar as a tourist destination. The clifftop paths not only allow you to look down on the red roofs of the buildings growing out of the coastal rock but also the sea air to permeate your lungs and blow away the cobwebs. This is as close to a bird's-eye view I could capture, if only we could soar above the landscape, taking in all its colour and splendour.

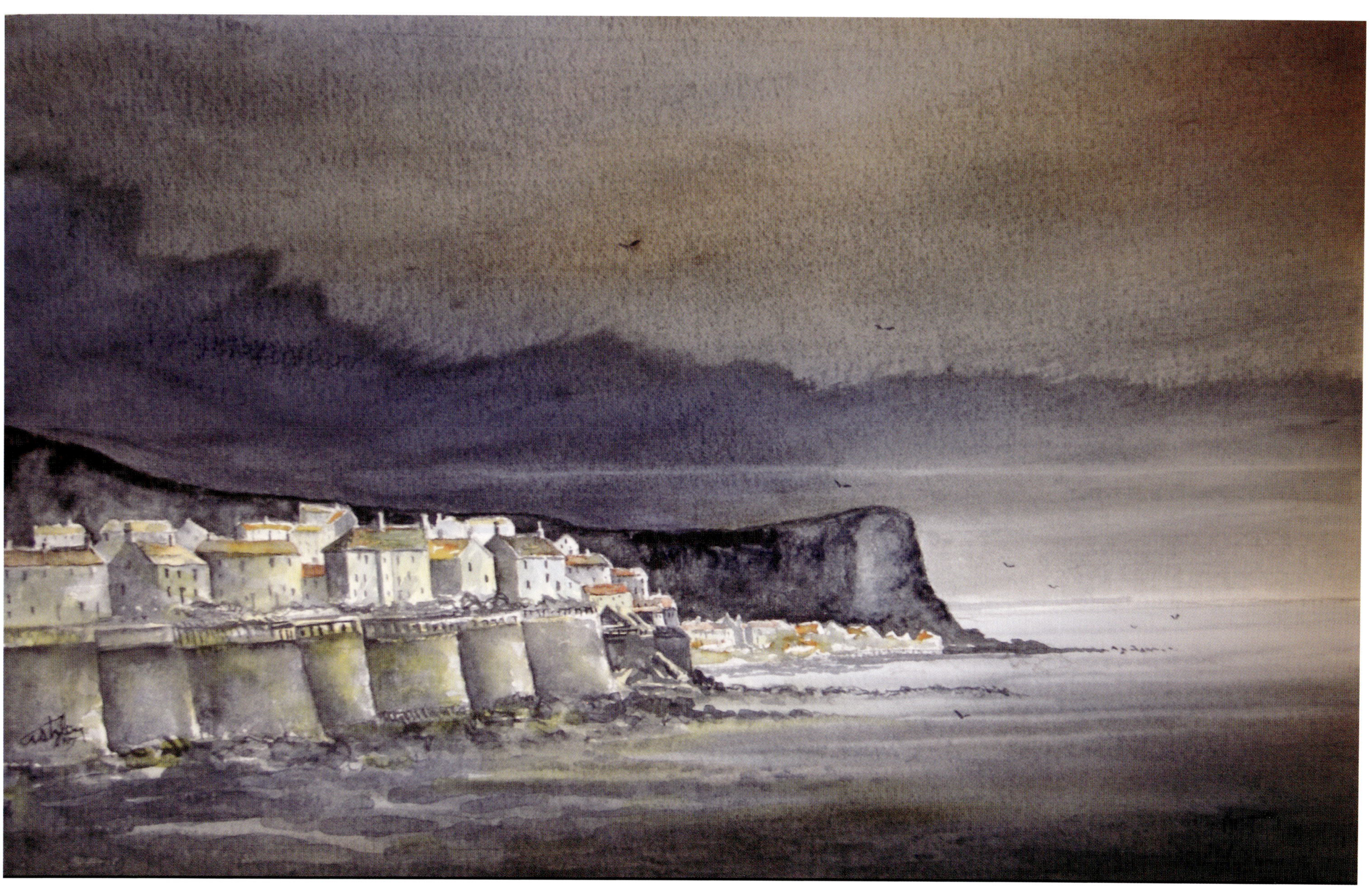

Cottages at Angram

Built in to the hillside, the farm buildings are partially protected from Nature's harsh winters. Look closely at the ground in front of the farm and you can see a reflection of the dark clouds passing overhead, it shows that reflections can occur on land as well as on water.

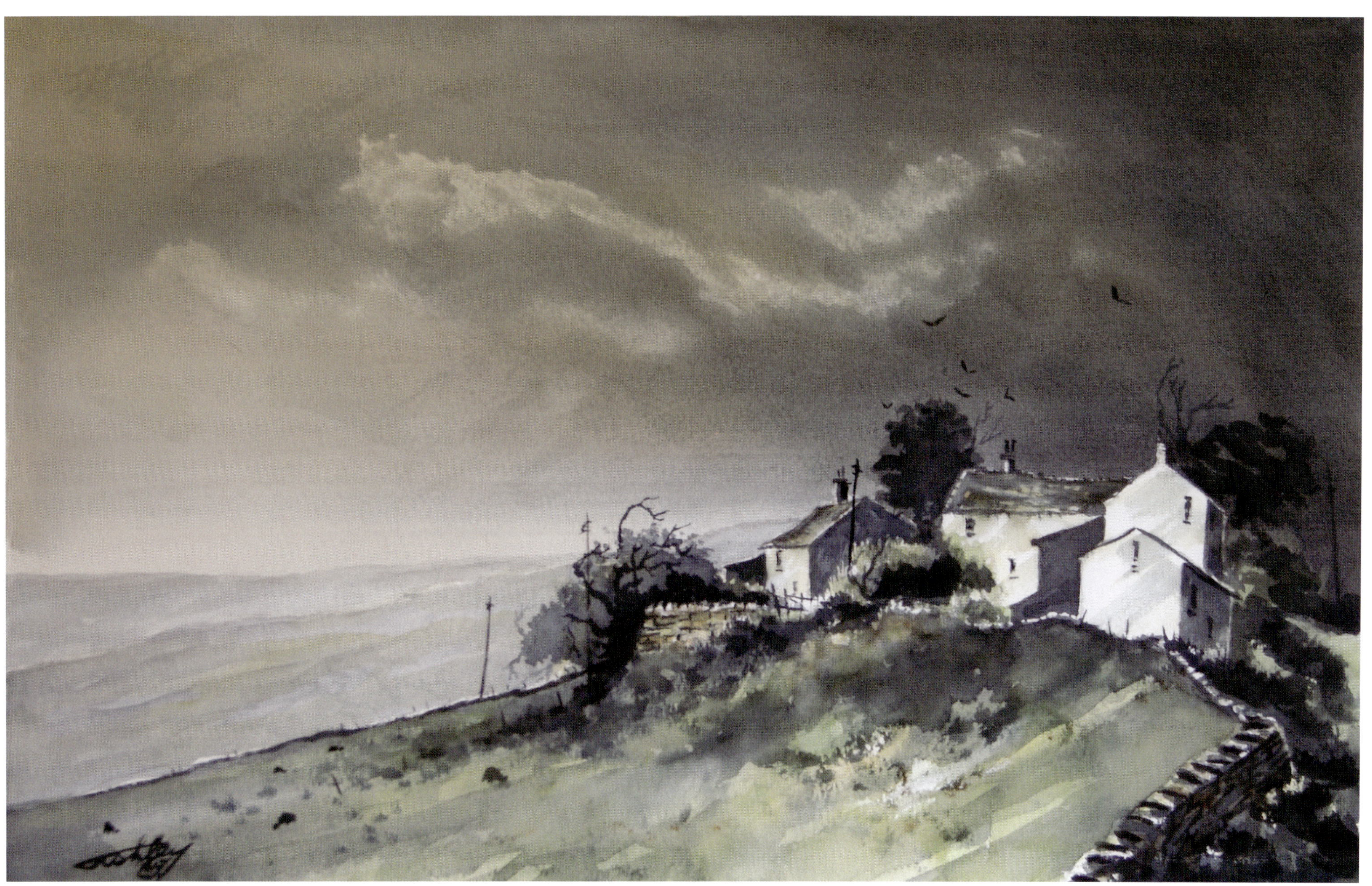

Bolster Moor – Snow

Snow shapes the landscape like a fresh white blanket thrown across a bed, cleaning the land and sharpening its contours. It is a crispness that allows you to see the moors with clear eyes.

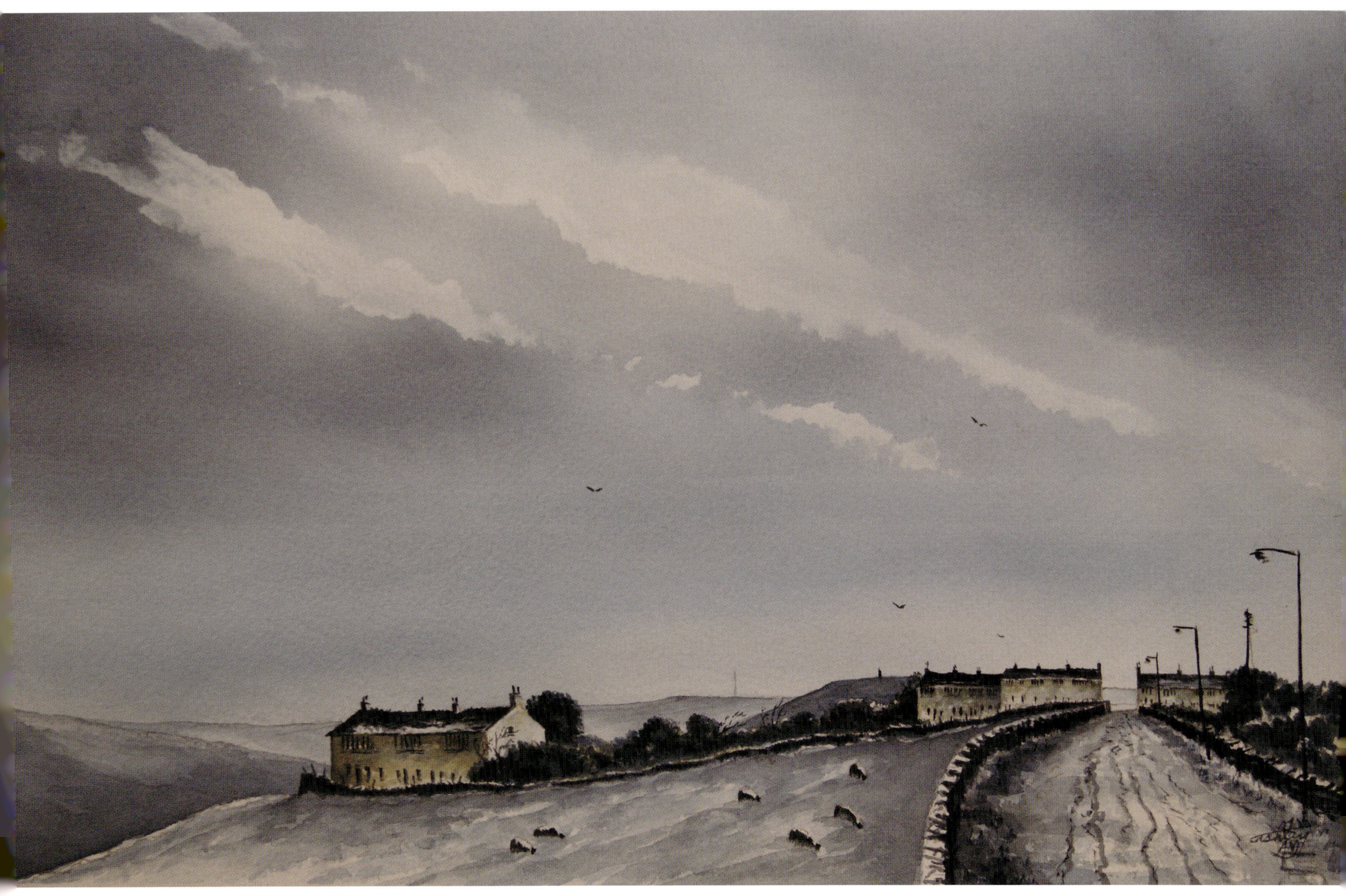

Bolster Moor – Snow   51

The Warmth of Heather – Castle Hill and Emley

Yorkshire has always been my mistress and capturing her ever-changing moods has given me everlasting pleasure.

I believe that painting requires two elements: the skill and the passion of the artist. Whereas you can be taught to paint a picture which is mechanically constructed, and you need to know about composition, perspective etc, to do a painting, but the most important attribute is to put your soul and passion in to the work: now you have a painting.

No one can teach you the passion that comes from within. You have to have a relationship with your subject. Mine is the Yorkshire Moor or my mistress as I like to call her, for her contours are those of the female form and just like a woman she can warm your heart, chill you to the bone or make you cry, such is the power of the elements and the atmosphere created.

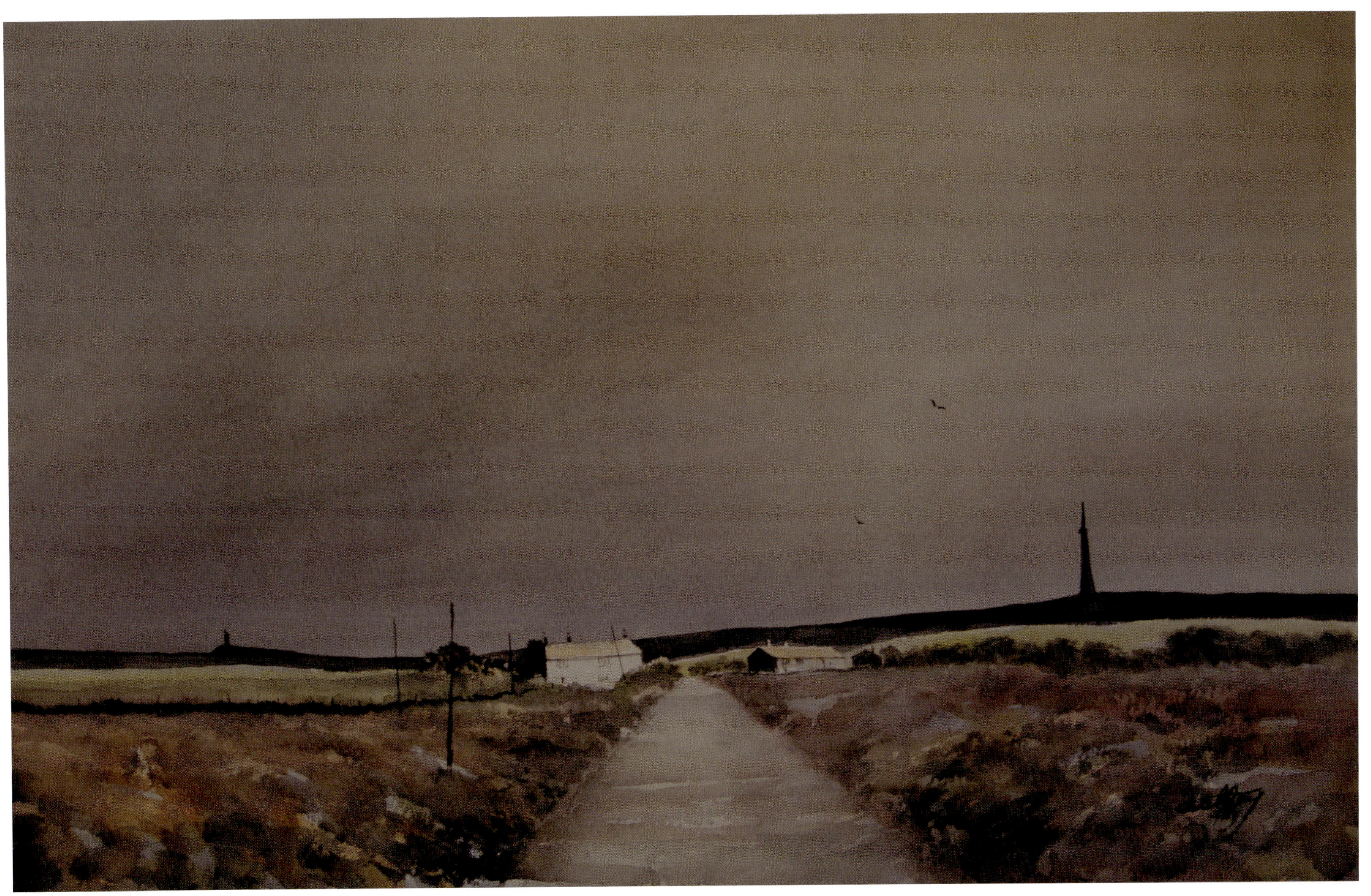

Storm Passing, New Mill

Like all moments in our lives, nature makes it easier to understand that the storm will pass and lighter skies will follow . . . if only life was so simple to understand . . .

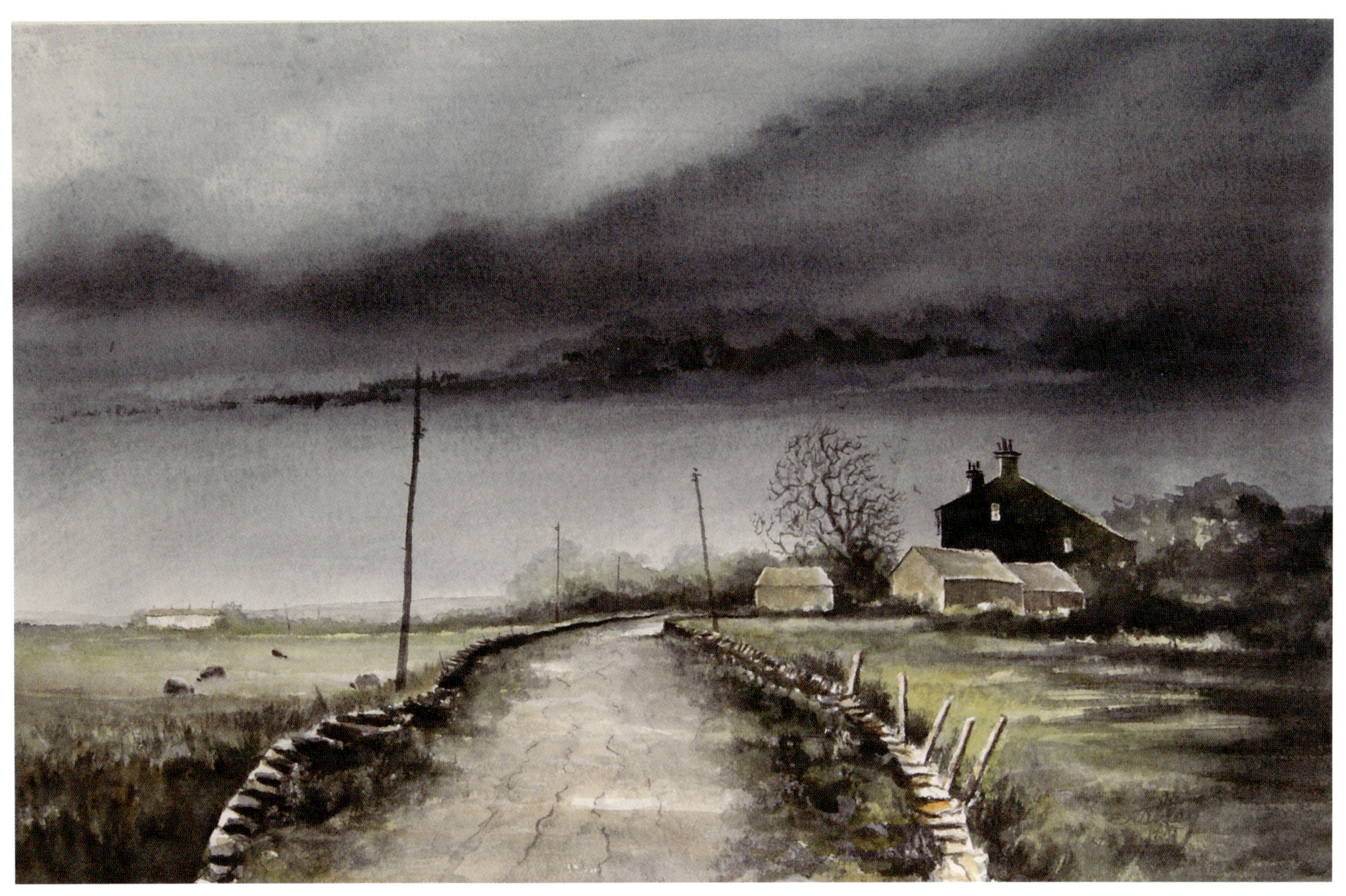

Calm after the Storm, Maythorne Moor

The snowstorm was over as soon as it had begun, arriving out of nowhere, leaving a blue sky with the warmth of evening sun in its wake. The farms huddle together in the distance in the same way that animals do for warmth, perhaps we have learnt something from nature after all . . .

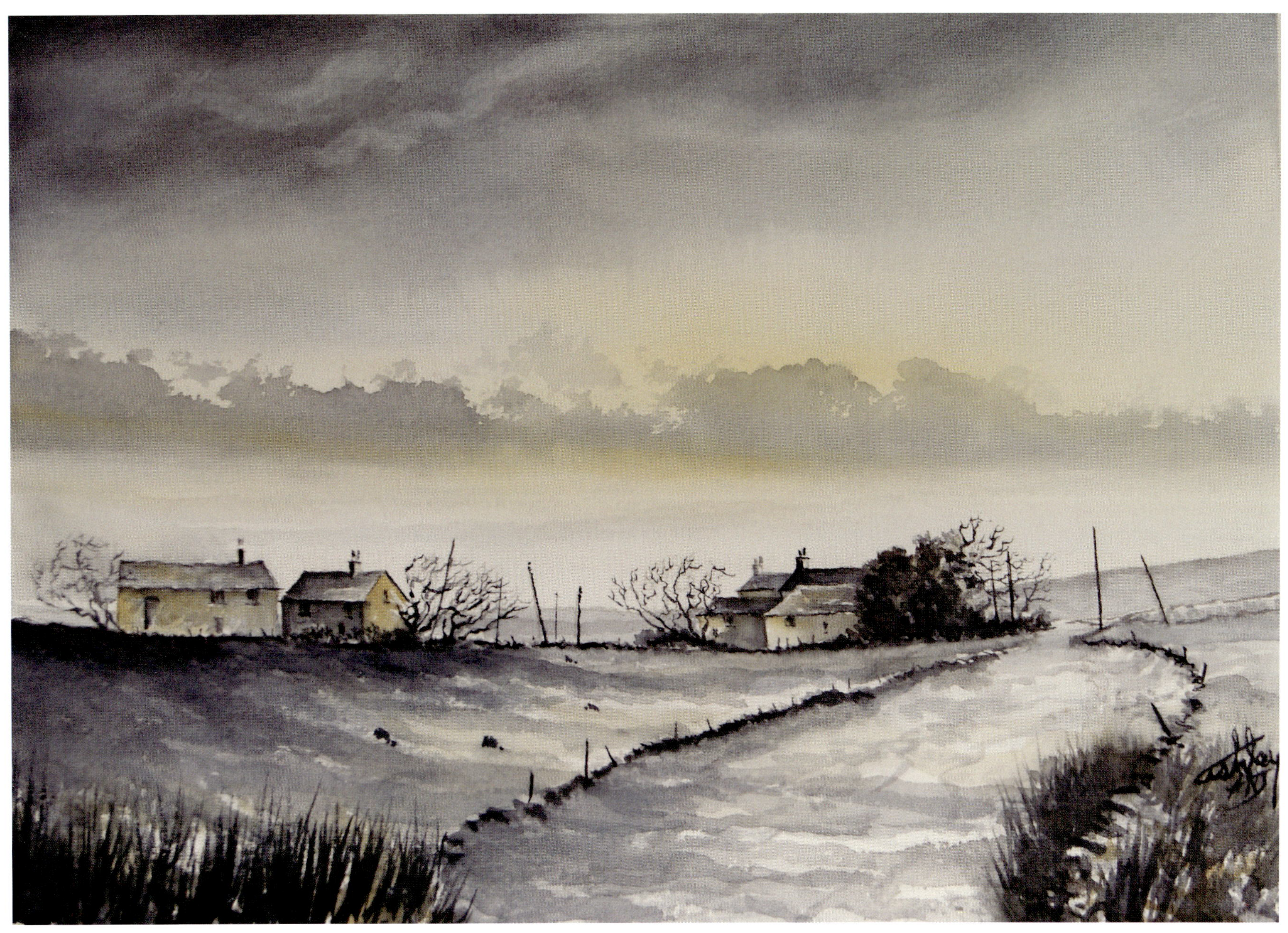

The Power of Nature
and its Beauty

On the way to Top Withens, Haworth. The house feels like it is the last stand; the boundary between civilization and Mother Nature, with the moorland stretching far beyond.

Like 'Alice through the Looking Glass', the sky created a kind of wormhole creating tunnel vision so only the farmhouse remains within the landscape.

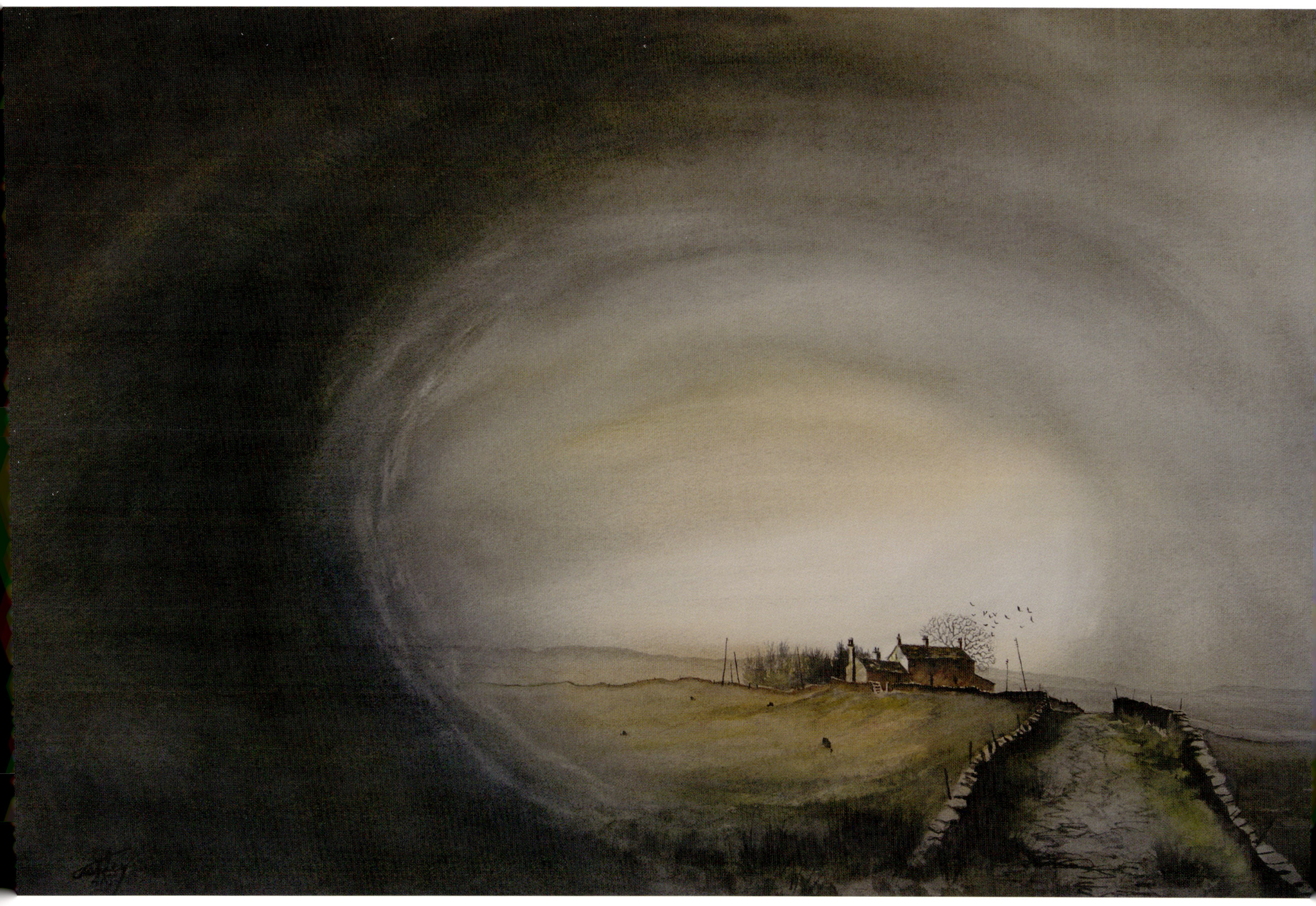

Bygone Days

Standing in the footsteps of the Brontës, with the house intact against the elements. Alas, although part of it still remains it cannot be restored to its former glory.

> *The soul, fortunately, has an interpreter – often an unconscious but still a faithful interpreter – in the eye.* (Charlotte Brontë, *Jane Eyre*)

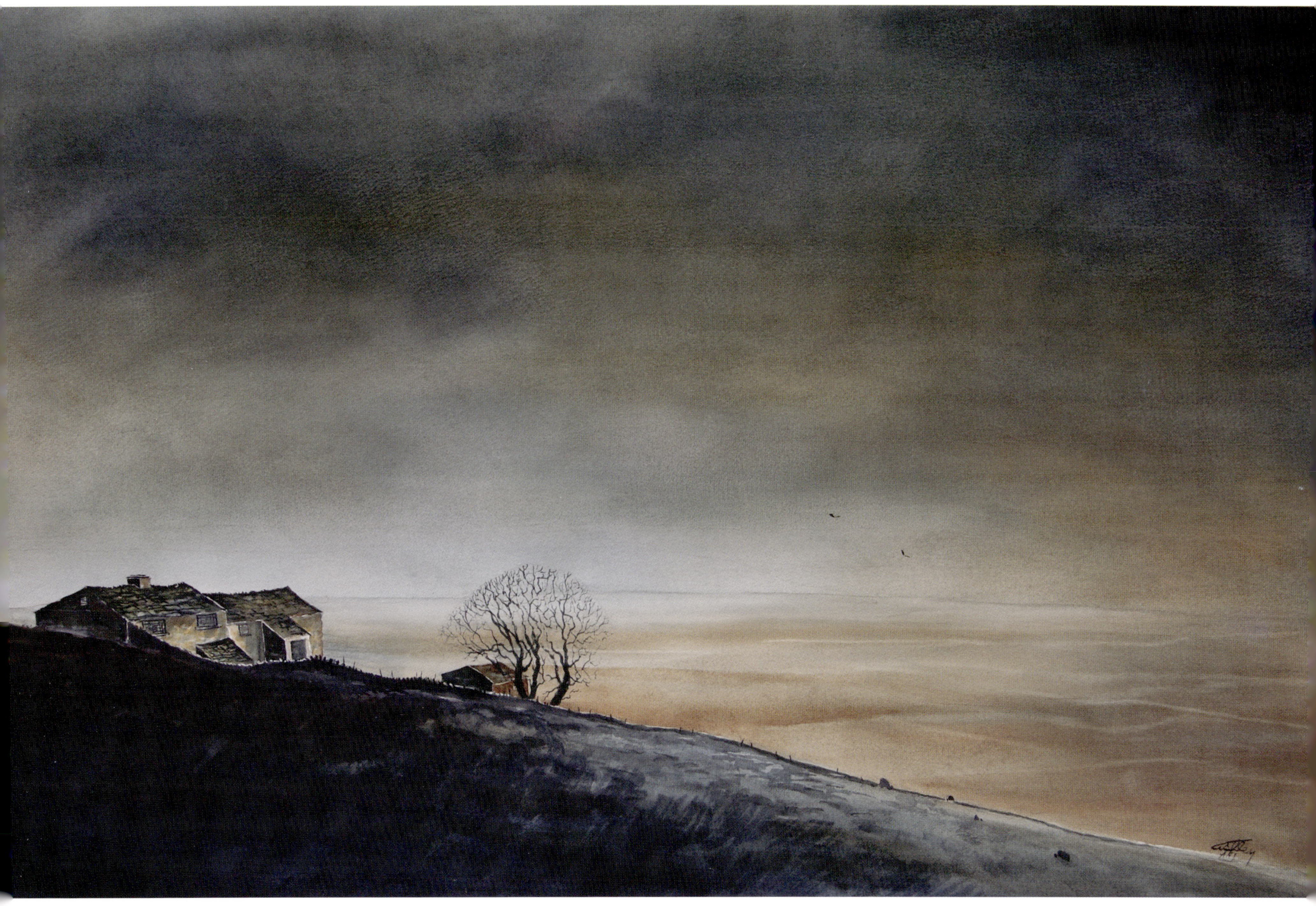

The End of the Day

The End Of The Day, When All is Calm is a celebration of my 75th year, with Castle Hill and Emley Moor in the distance but with the moorland farm protectively built into the hillside it gives an insight into how far man has come in technology but yet where nature prevails, the old ways are still the best.

The late afternoon sun casts its final rays of burnt sienna across the valley, leaving a deceptive feeling of warmth on the snow-covered landscape it touches. But this is Yorkshire: sunshine in the rain, blizzards on a sunny day, weather that is often hard to read . . . for this I am fortunate, for my enduring love affair with Yorkshire has enabled me to sense her moods and impending drama.

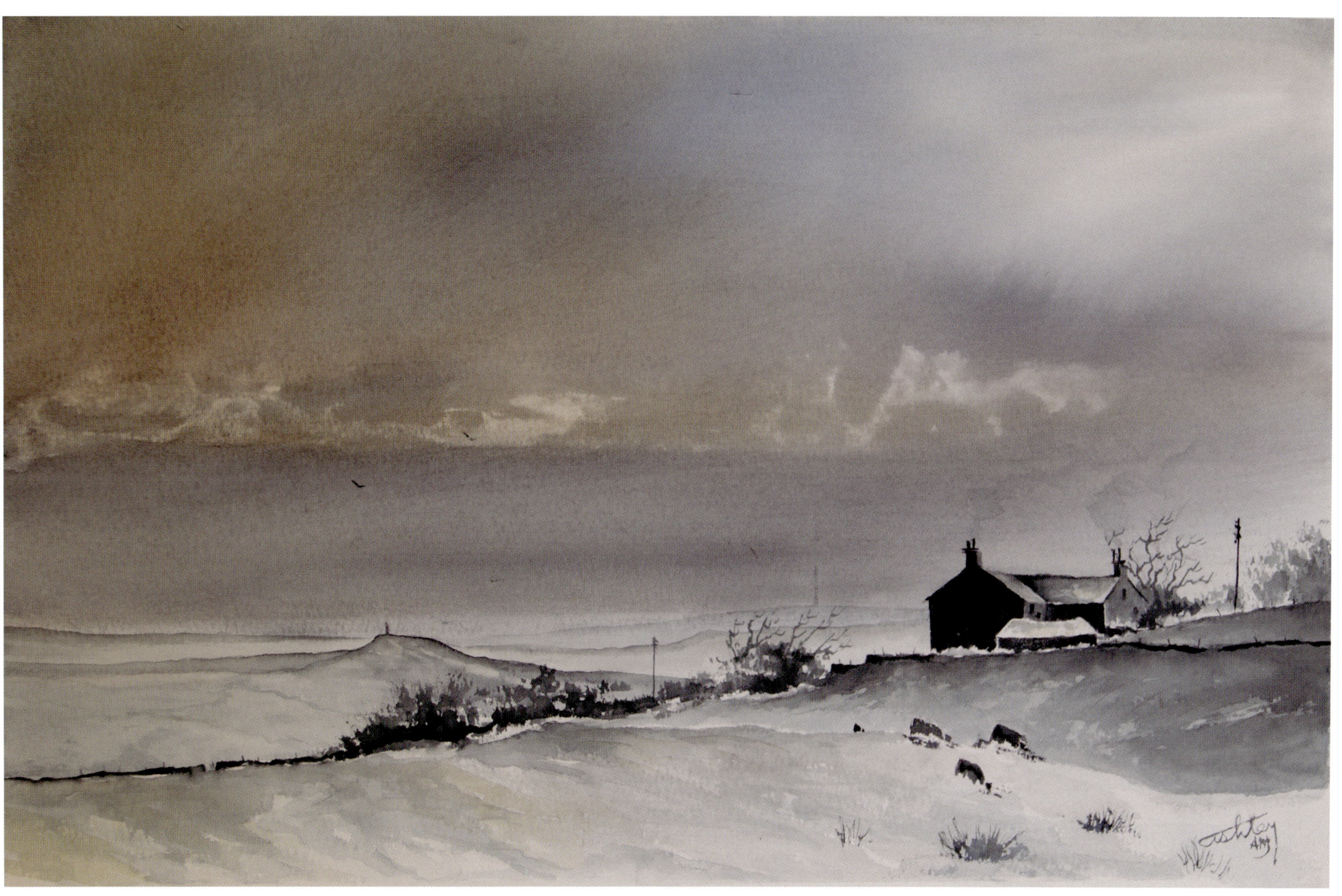

The Close of the Day when Evening Light Descends

To be alone with your thoughts on the open moor is not the same as loneliness or isolation, for my muse and mistress is always with me from the moment I open my eyes to resting my head at the end of the day, for she is carried within my heart and soul.

I know we are herd people,
we feel safe in a crowd,
But I am one who feels at one
with the Moor, alone.
Yet I never feel alone
when I paint with the music of the wind
and the tears of the rain
that touch my face with joy.
(Ashley Jackson, 1999)

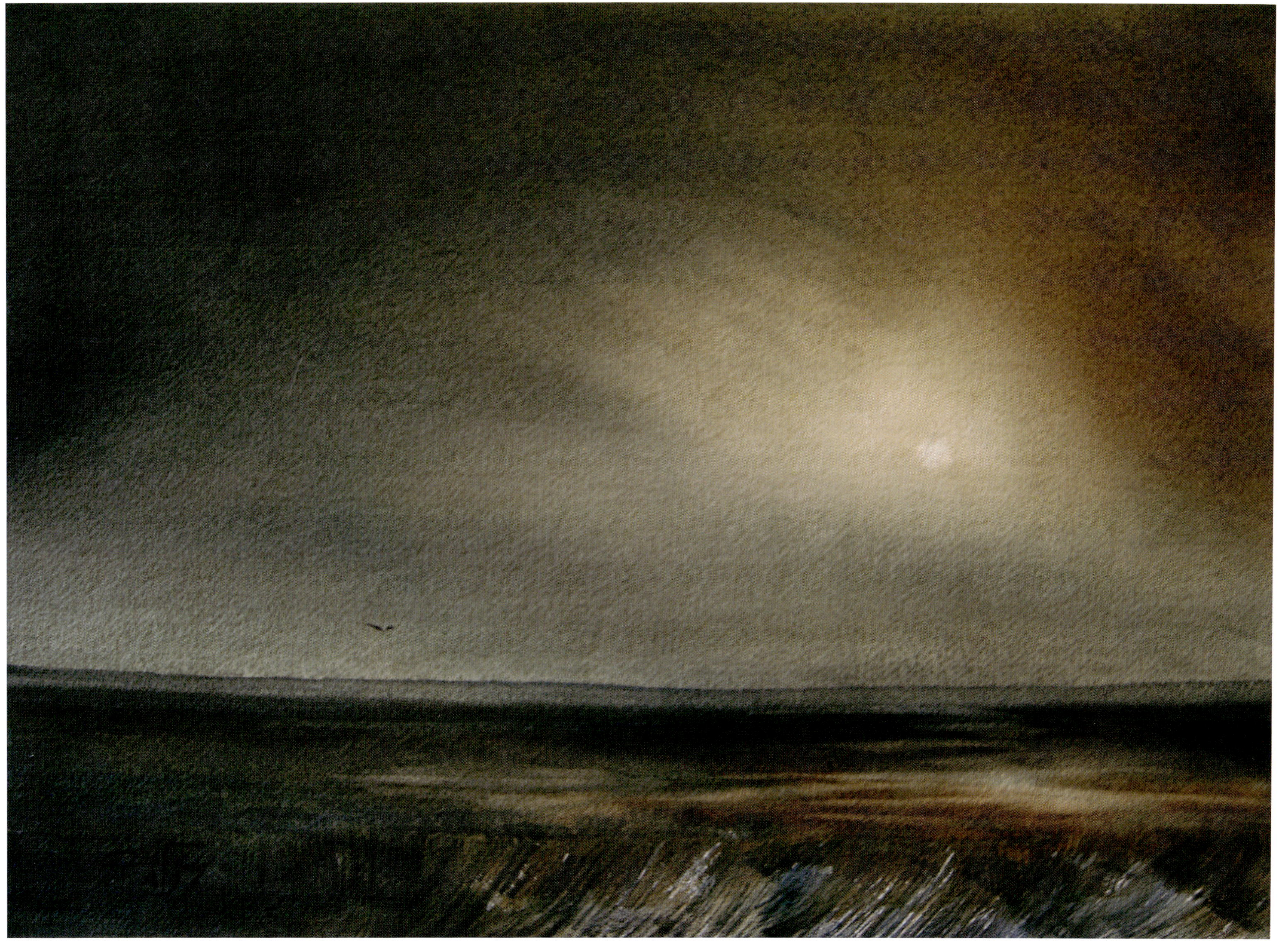

The Sun Rises on a New Day

I have attempted to capture the peace and tranquillity of Swaledale. Sometimes you can be forgiven in to thinking that for a brief moment in time the world has stopped to allow you to absorb the softness of the landscape, the sheep grazing and birds in flight, taking it in with all your senses . . . and then it's back to real life.

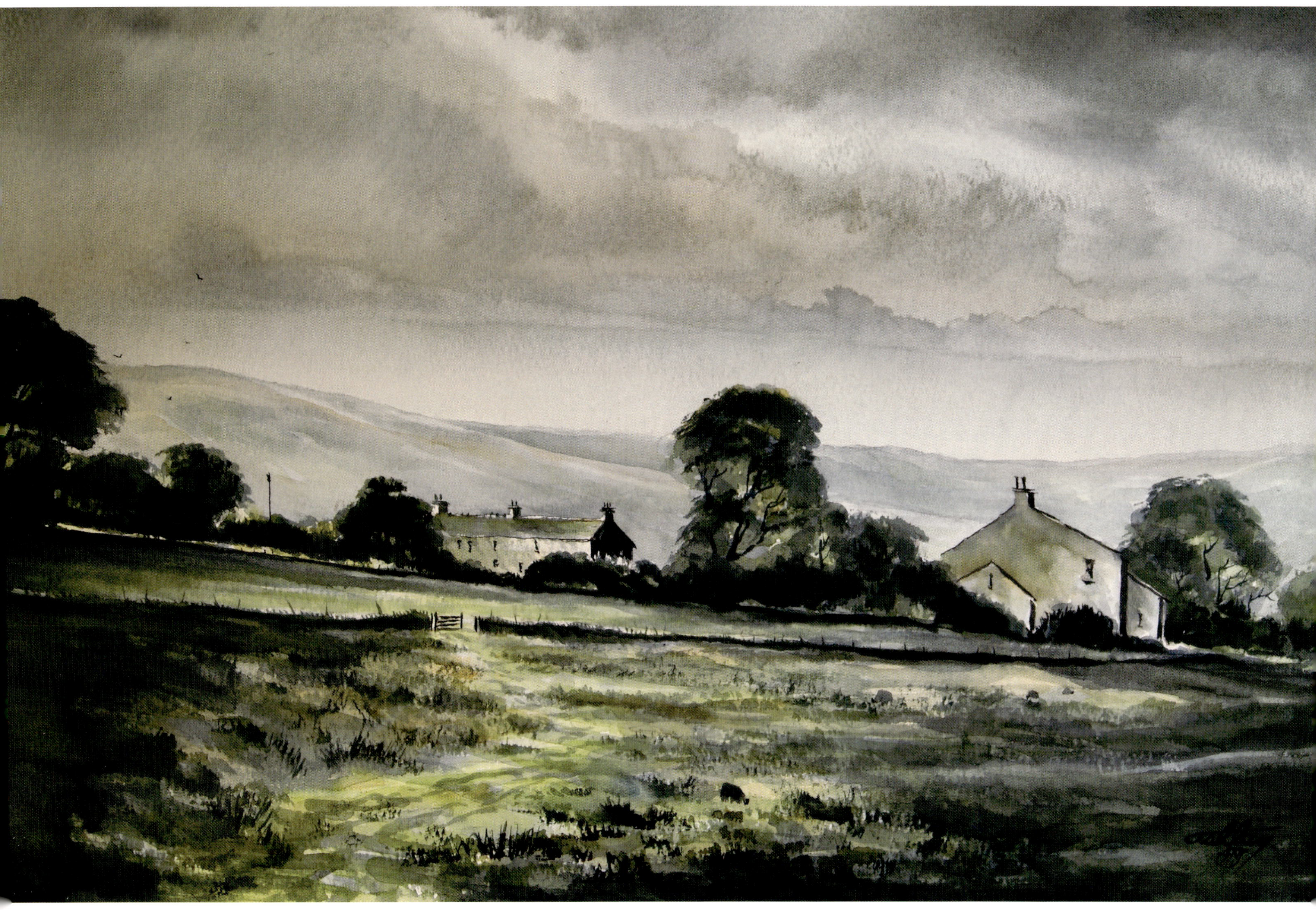

Coming Home Before the Rain

As I stood on the Brontë moorland with the storm approaching, I could sense her turmoil and taste her tears: the gate in front of me was open as if inviting me to walk down the path and reach the sanctuary of the farmhouse. I chose instead to do the exact opposite of what she was telling me, I proceeded to get out my paints to capture the changing light and the drama of the occasion. The impending rain did not threaten me, for I was home and at peace with my Yorkshire mistress.

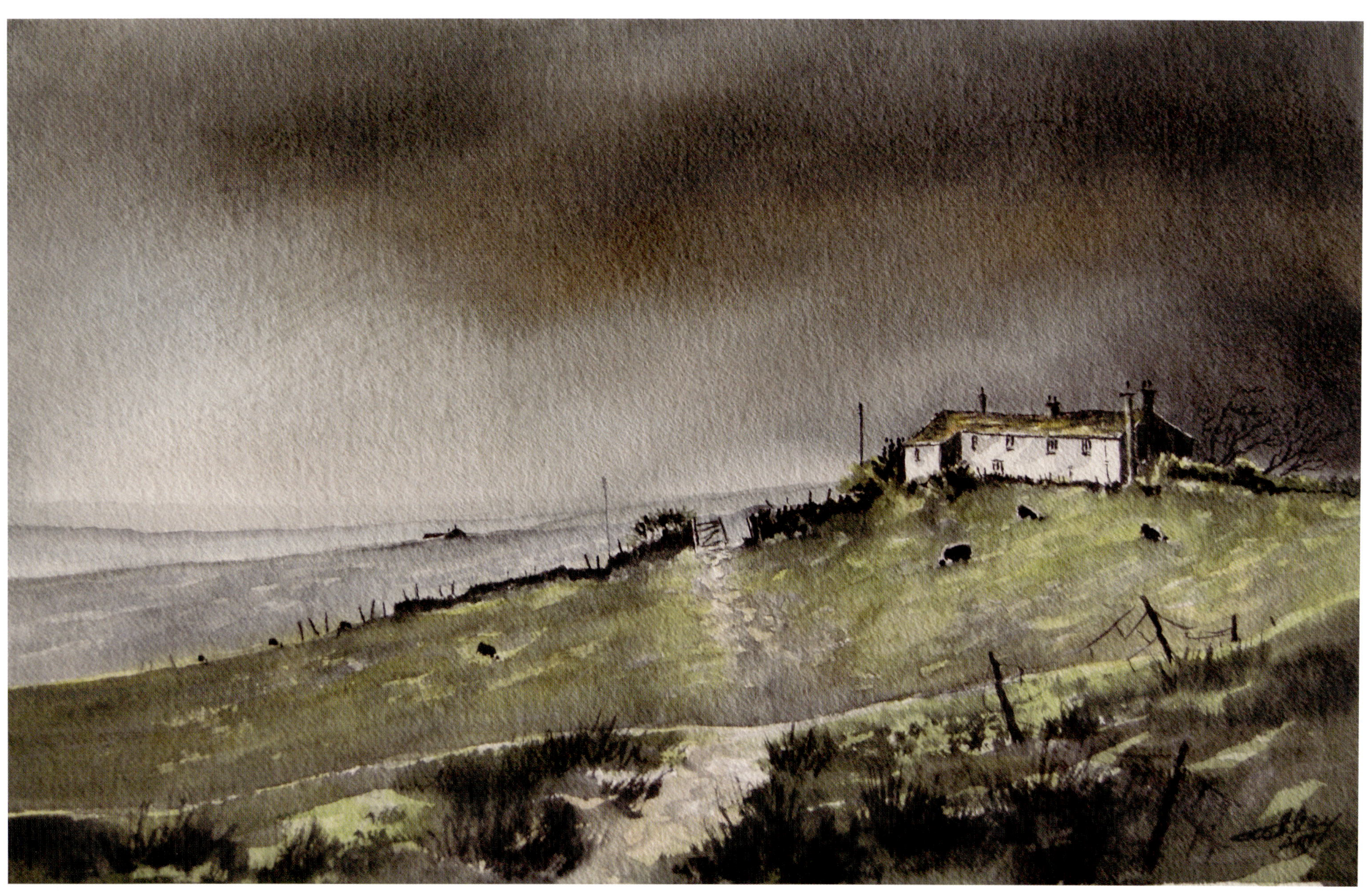

Meltham in the Snow

'Landmarks of our lives'. Looking down to Meltham from West Nab with the majestic monuments of Castle Hill and Emley Moor Mast standing proud against the skyline.

There are three iconic landmarks in the Holme Valley: Castle Hill, a monument built in celebration of Queen Victoria's Jubilee, Emley Mast and Holme Moss Mast, creating a triangle between them. Once within sight, the heart heralds a homecoming.

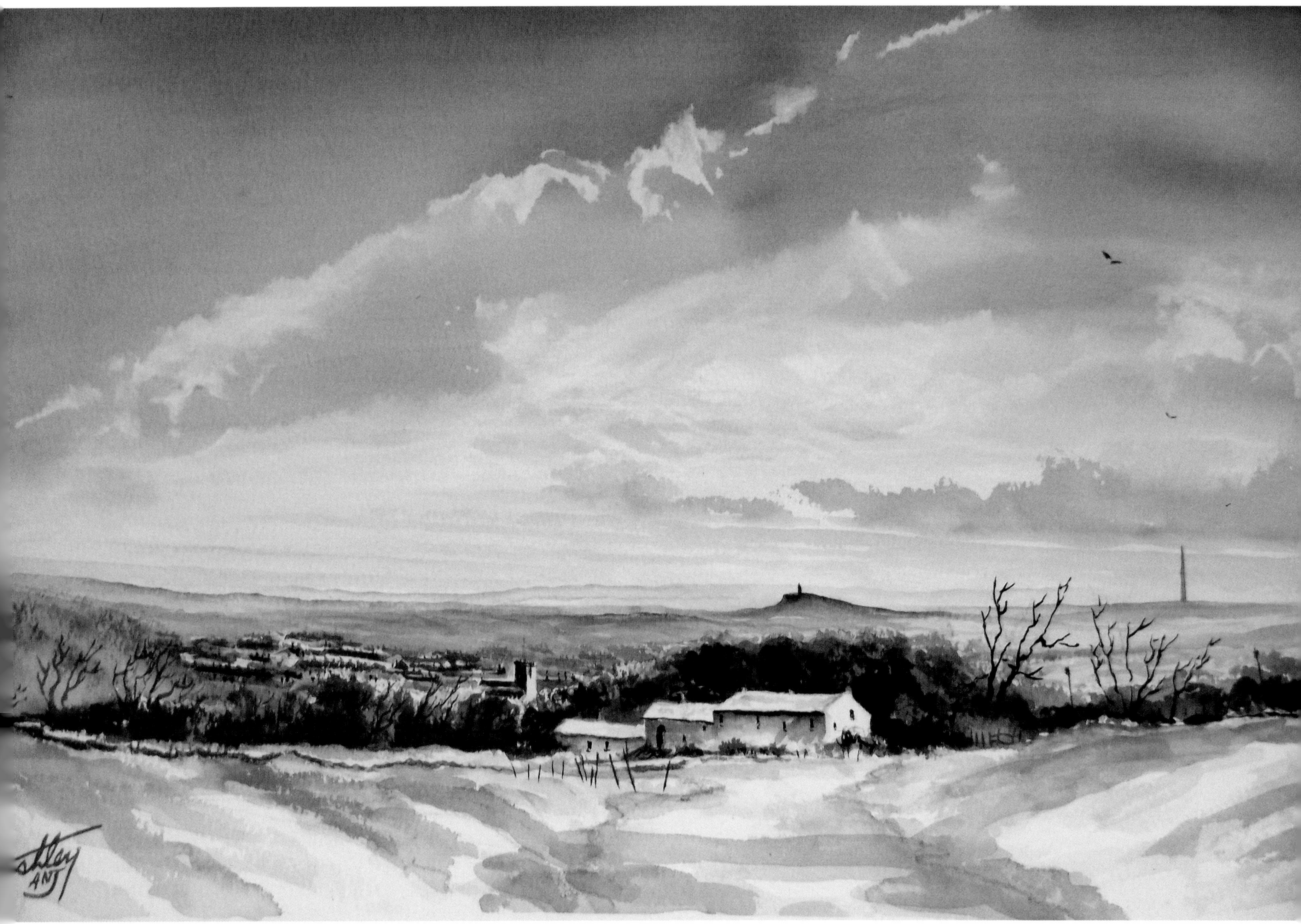

The Red Postbox – Yockenthwaite

Tilting on a weathered wooden post, the red postbox acts like a beacon in the landscape, a connection between the hamlet of Yockenthwaite and the outside world. Furthermore, the dry stone bridge over the river is a natural but also perhaps an imaginary boundary which one must cross to reach the idyllic rural life of the Langstrothdale Valley. It conjures up the romantic notion of packing up urban life and making a living off the land, an image that is far removed from reality.

This is probably the most photographed postbox in the country, for it is both isolated and idyllic in its charm.

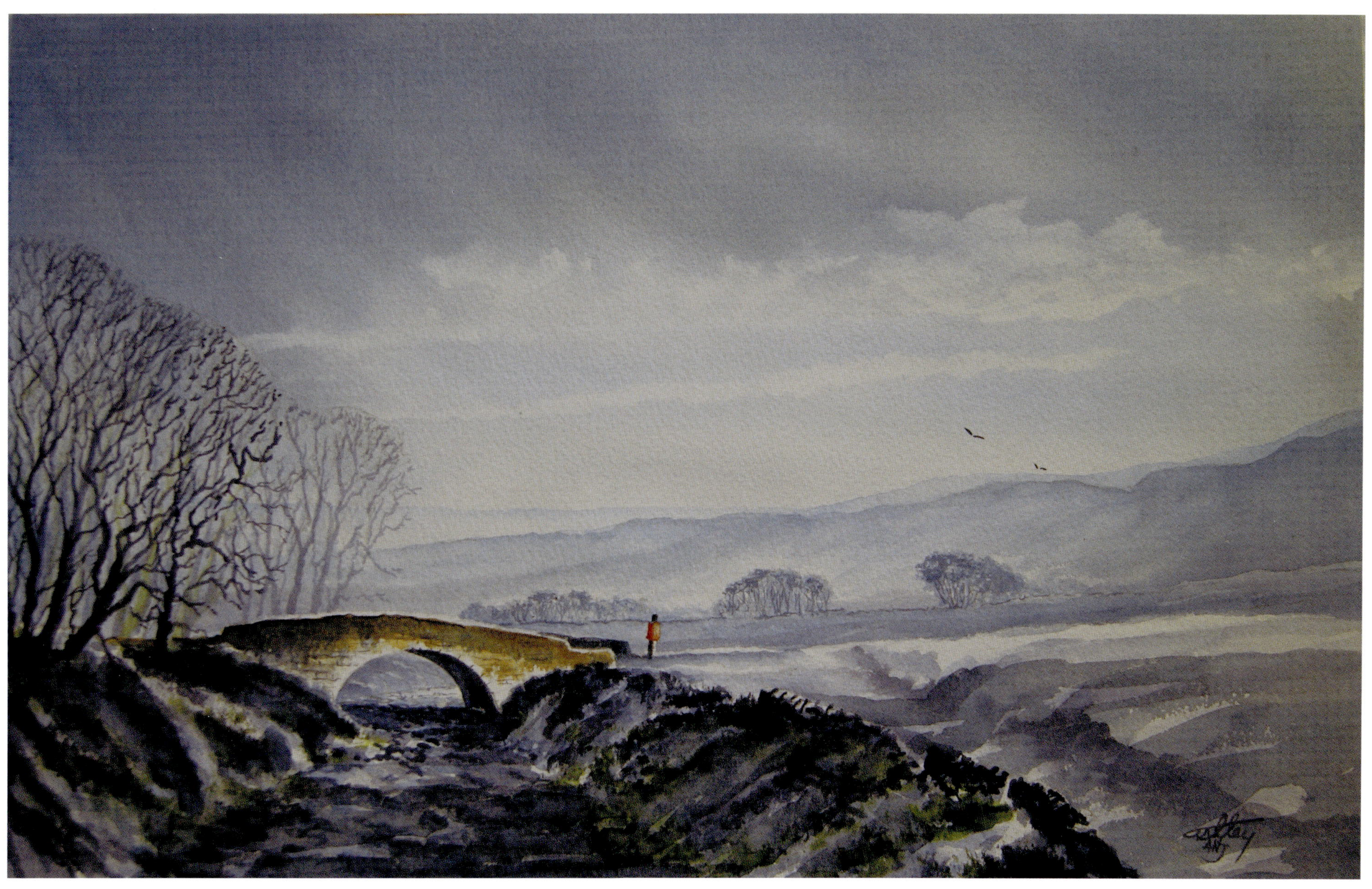

Low Row, Swaledale

The peace and tranquillity of Swaledale has been truly captured in the hamlet of farmhouses, with the afternoon sun lighting up the embankment of trees. You feel as if you could walk right into village life, such is its welcome.

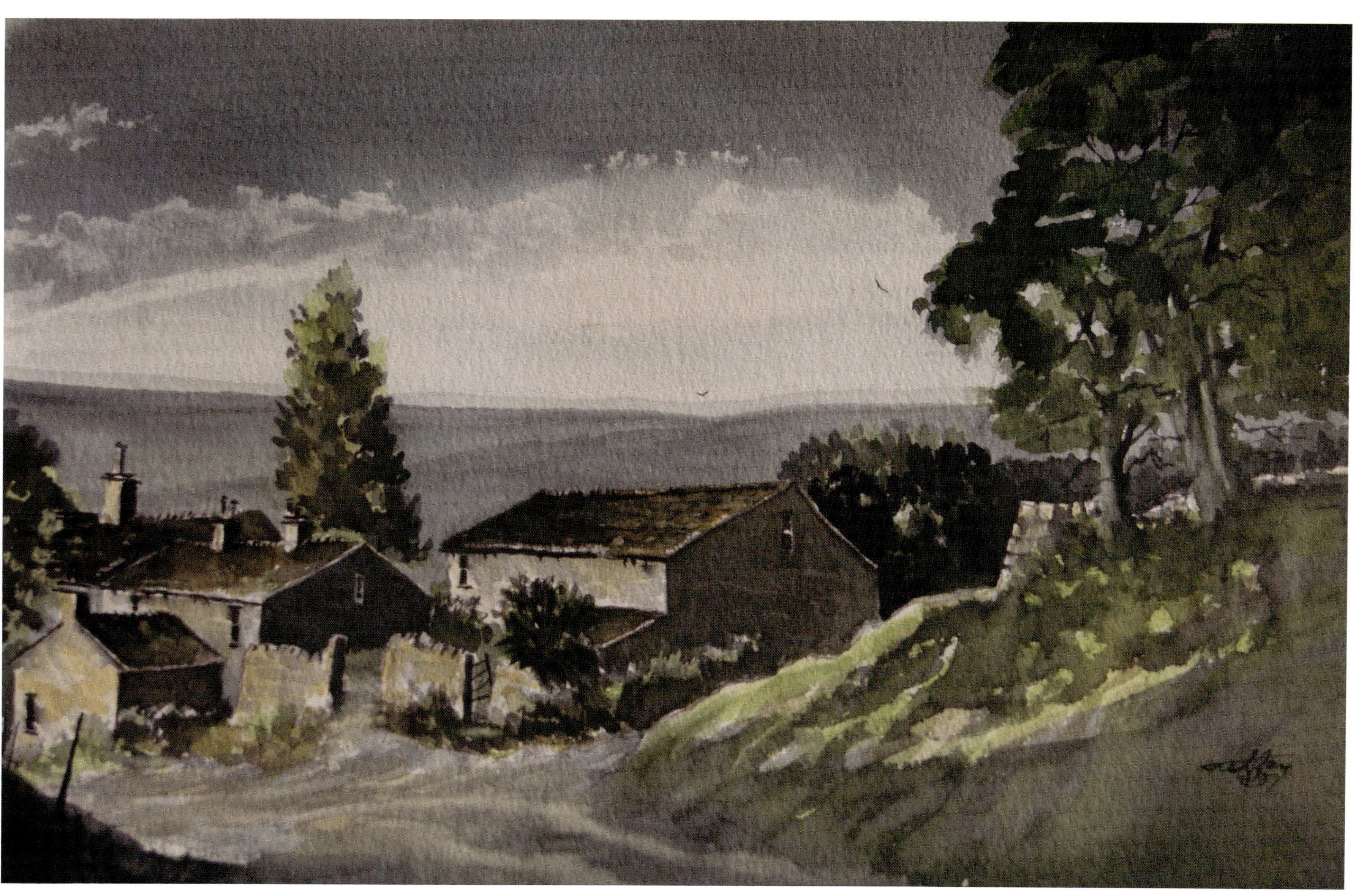

Hill Top Farm going down to Meltham from West Nab

As a boy of 9 years old, my eyes were opened to this unforgettable landscape with Castle Hill in the distance, I had been to visit the Cock Crowing stone on Marsden Moor on the way out of Meltham. To this day I am still unsure of why it was given this name… but it still exists, as does my love of this breathtaking view: it will remain with me for the rest of my life.

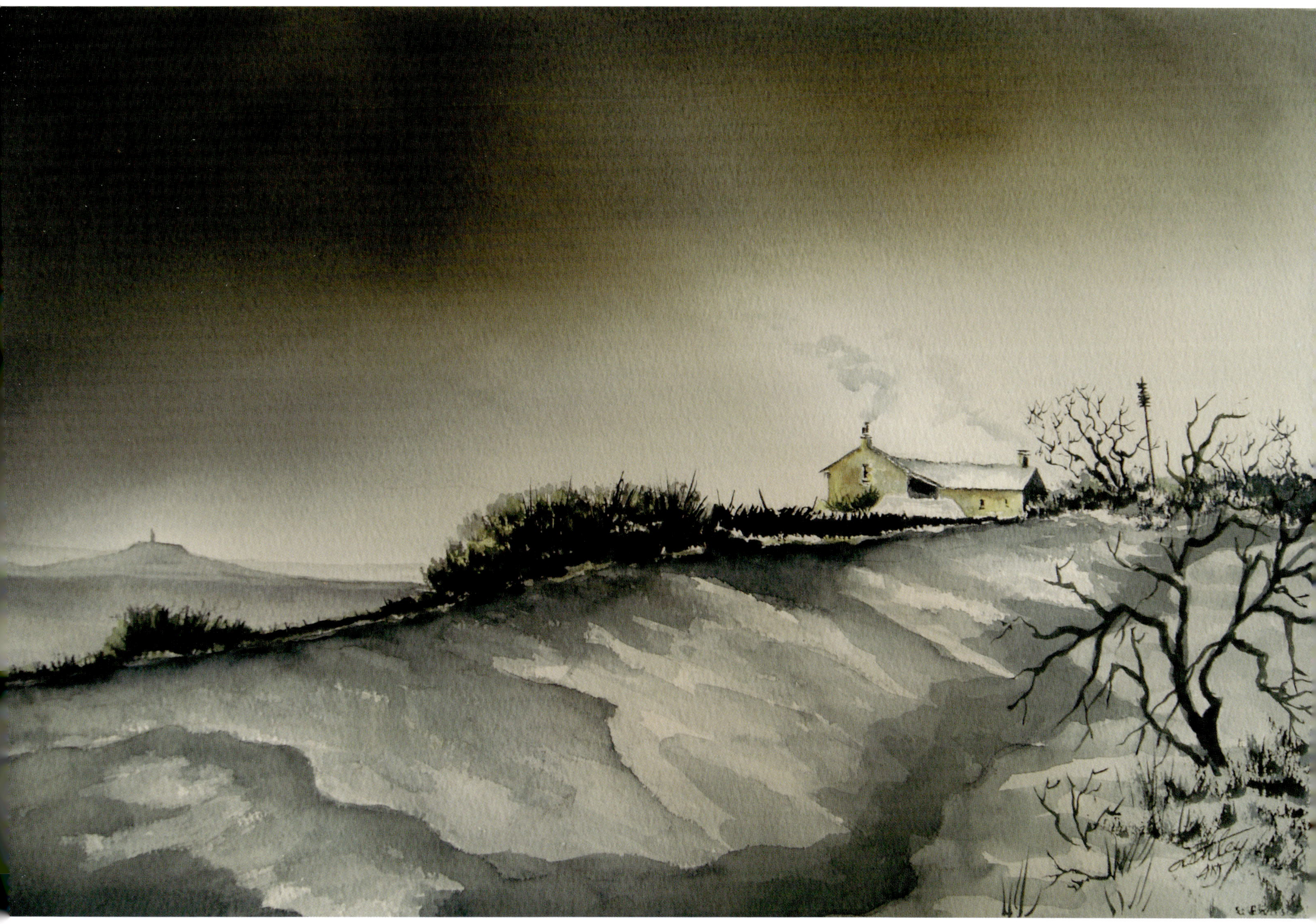

Reflections of Skies – West Nab

This is true serenity, where the sky and moorland work in harmony, reflecting the colours of the landscape into the sky like a mirror image. With Deer Hill and West Nab in the distance, the remaining gatepost and dry stone wall, although no longer complete, make you feel that you should pass through the man-made opening out of respect rather than head for the open moorland.

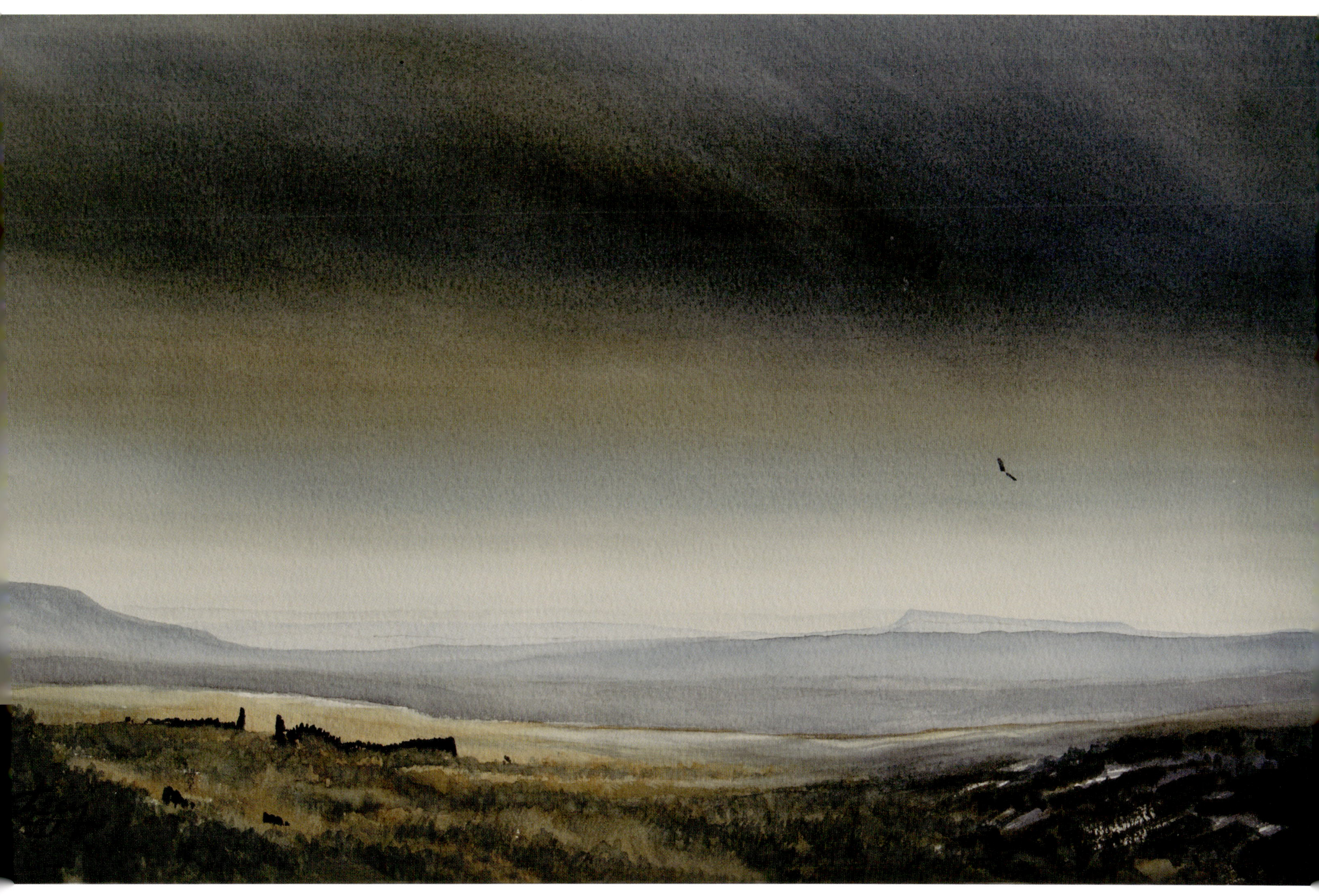

The Road Less Travelled

Remembering winters past when the wall toppings were the only visible clue remaining that a road or pathway was hidden underneath the deep snow.

Here footprints in the fresh snow lead us to and from the hamlet, I can only imagine that on these days it must be majestic to be a bird soaring above the landscape into the clear blue sky with nothing but white beneath you, with the wall toppings marking out the land divisions like a patchwork quilt.

Each year I personally chose a painting to reproduce as a Christmas card . . . this was chosen to be the Christmas card for 2016. Little did I know at the time how symbolic the title would become to us all.

Two roads diverged in a yellow wood,
And sorry I could not travel both
And be one traveller, long I stood
And looked down one as far as I could
To where it bent in the undergrowth;

Then took the other, as just as fair,
And having perhaps the better claim
Because it was grassy and wanted wear,
Though as for that the passing there
Had worn them really about the same,

And both that morning equally lay
In leaves no step had trodden black.
Oh, I kept the first for another day!
Yet knowing how way leads on to way
I doubted if I should ever come back.

I shall be telling this with a sigh
Somewhere ages and ages hence:
Two roads diverged in a wood, and I,
I took the one less travelled by,
And that has made all the difference.
(Robert Frost – *The Road Not Taken*, 1920)

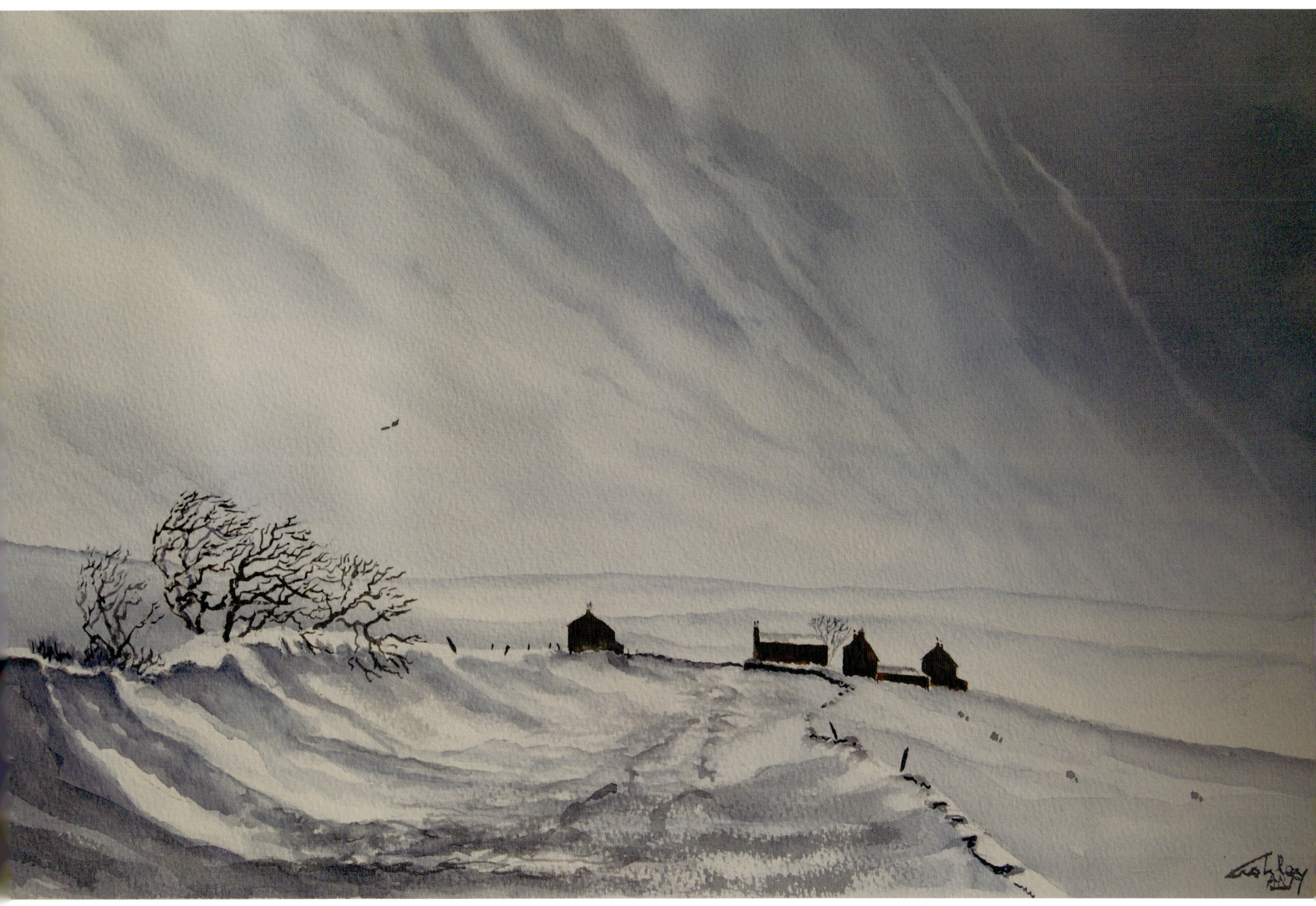

I Feel the Power

Although I stand alone on the moors, I am never alone nor do I feel isolated, for I am with my love and mistress – Yorkshire. I am fortunate to have shared my life and emotions with her and she with me. For it is on rare days like this that I get to glimpse the raw atmosphere of the moors and even now after all these years it still humbles me.

Yorkshire has really got a strong hold of me.
But why should I let her go
And where would I be if she was not there.
(Ashley Jackson, 1970)

When Winter Moves In – Bolster Moor

The view from the hamlet of Bolster Moor is a great reference as to how high the land really is, for the flat landscape could be deceptive to the eye until you turn to view the unfolding panorama in front of you, with the iconic Castle Hill and Emley Mast visible on a clear day. On this day the storm clouds were building, creating a dark sense of impending drama whilst the wind was to dictate whether the Jubilee Tower was to become a lighthouse in the eye of the storm.

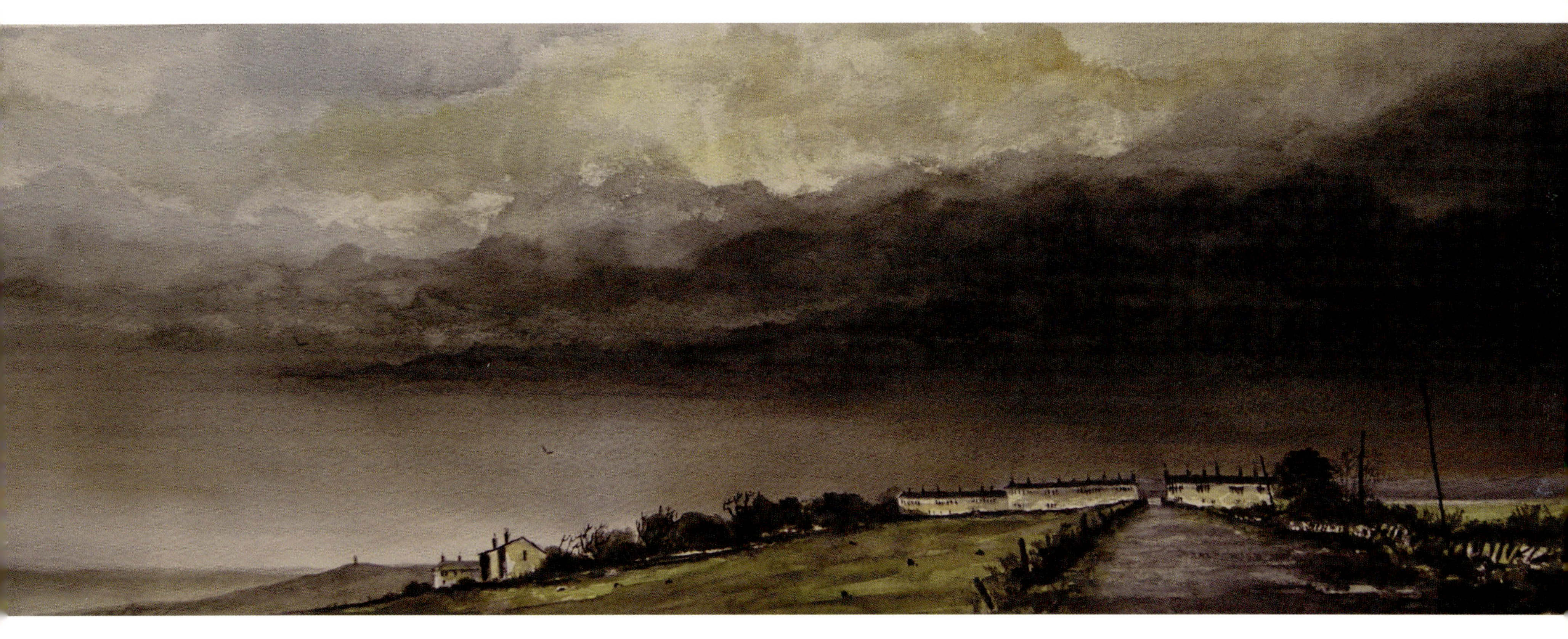

When Winter Moves In – Bolster Moor   85

Buttertubs Pass

Buttertubs Pass: this great road takes us to the heart of the Yorkshire Dales, rated by Jeremy Clarkson as 'England's only truly spectacular road' and in 2014 it was a dramatic backdrop to the Tour de France Grand Depart first day. Ascending the challenging pass from the south in Hawes before reaching exposed moorland and the true summit of 526 metres.

The name Buttertubs comes from the limestone potholes formed by the rock face at the side of the road. Local legend suggests that farmers would use them to store their butter during the summer en route to market.

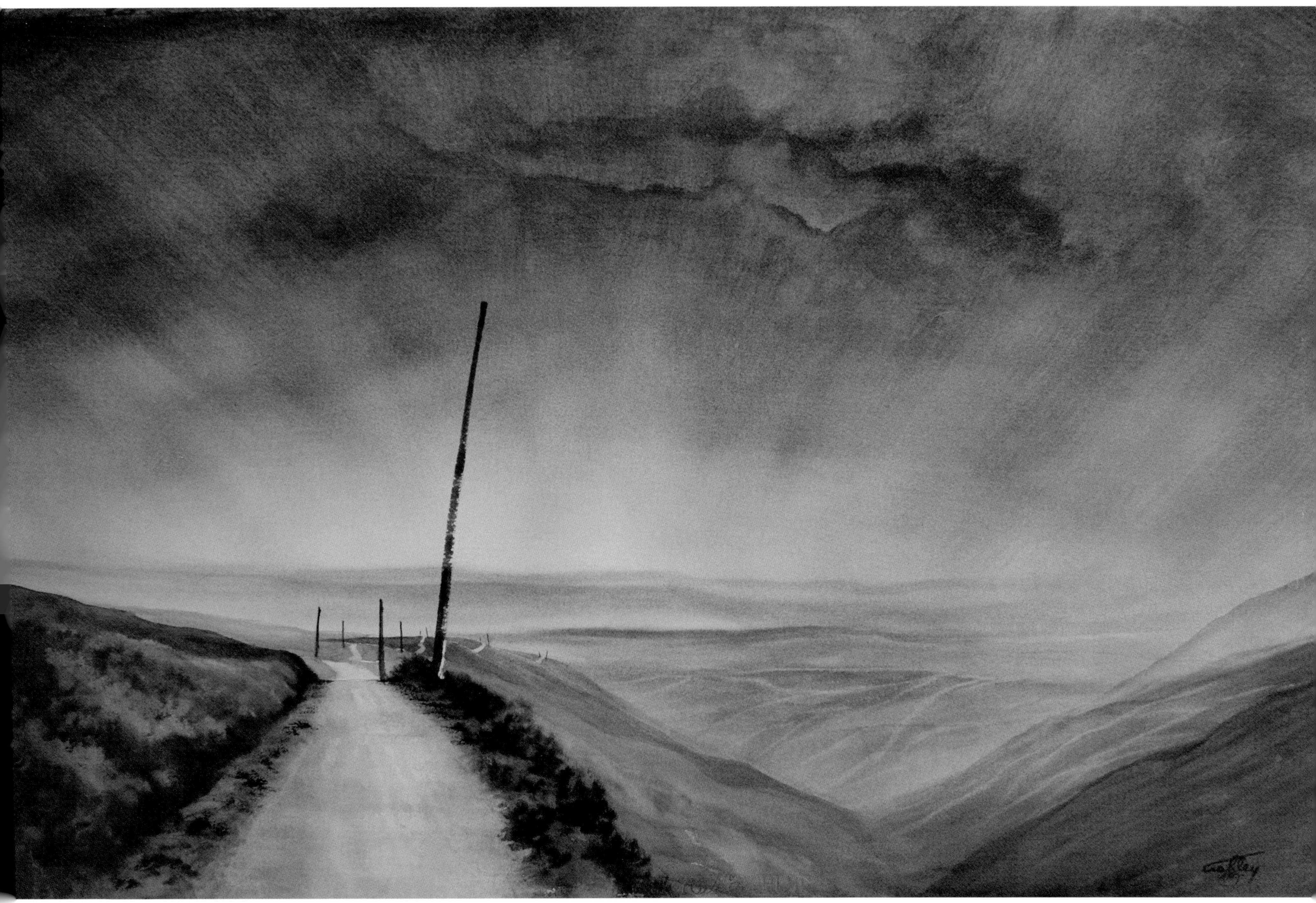

Kidstone Pass

All my life I have always been criticized about 'where is the sunshine, where are the bright colours'? My answer is when I was 16 and at art school, I wrote in my diary 'I do not want to be the genius of the chocolate box'.

When I stand upon the moors I cannot paint what I don't feel, thus there are days and weeks when I cannot paint. I have to wait until I feel the hair on the back of my neck stand on end and I get a 'wow' feeling. Something else has to connect rather than just the visual senses.

As a professional artist for over fifty years I hope that Art will find a way back to skills and passion rather than technicians and clinicians: if you were writing a letter to a loved one would you not want to write it personally rather than have someone else dictate it for you?

Perhaps I am a romantic at heart . . . but Art has been hijacked by the pseudo-intellectuals, telling others what they should like.

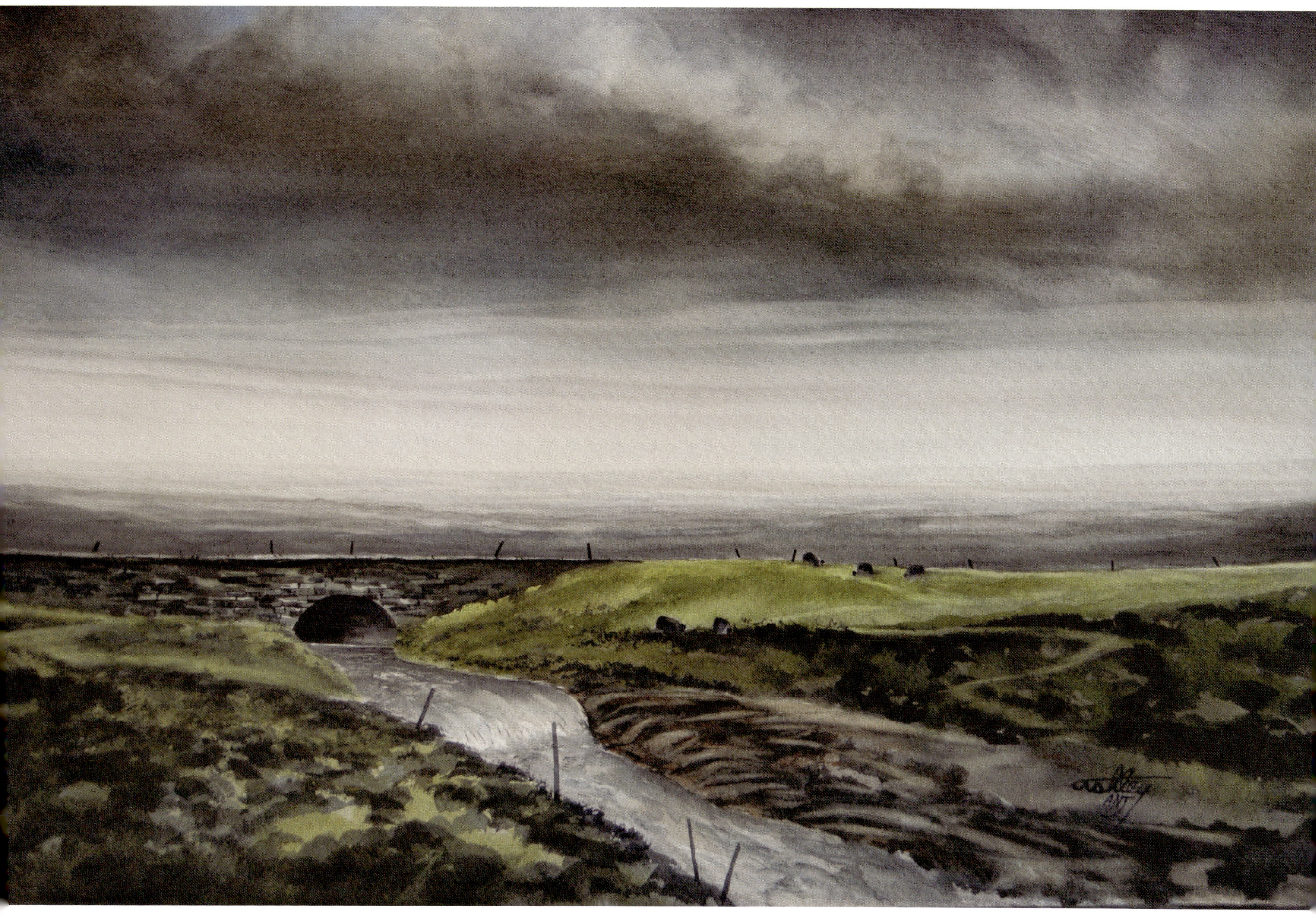

Langsett Moor, North America

There are various stories of why North America Farm came to be named as such. It is most likely, however, that it is due to the tradition of naming some outlying farms after what were at that time considered remote parts of the world. It is so easy to forget how big the world must have seemed before the advent of aeroplanes and how many New World settlers died on their way to America.

> *The large mullions and pillars lay like fallen headstones in tribute to those who were filled with determination or as we say 'Yorkshire grit' in trying to carve a living balancing the fine line between nature and nurture in such an unforgiving landscape.*
> (Ashley Jackson)

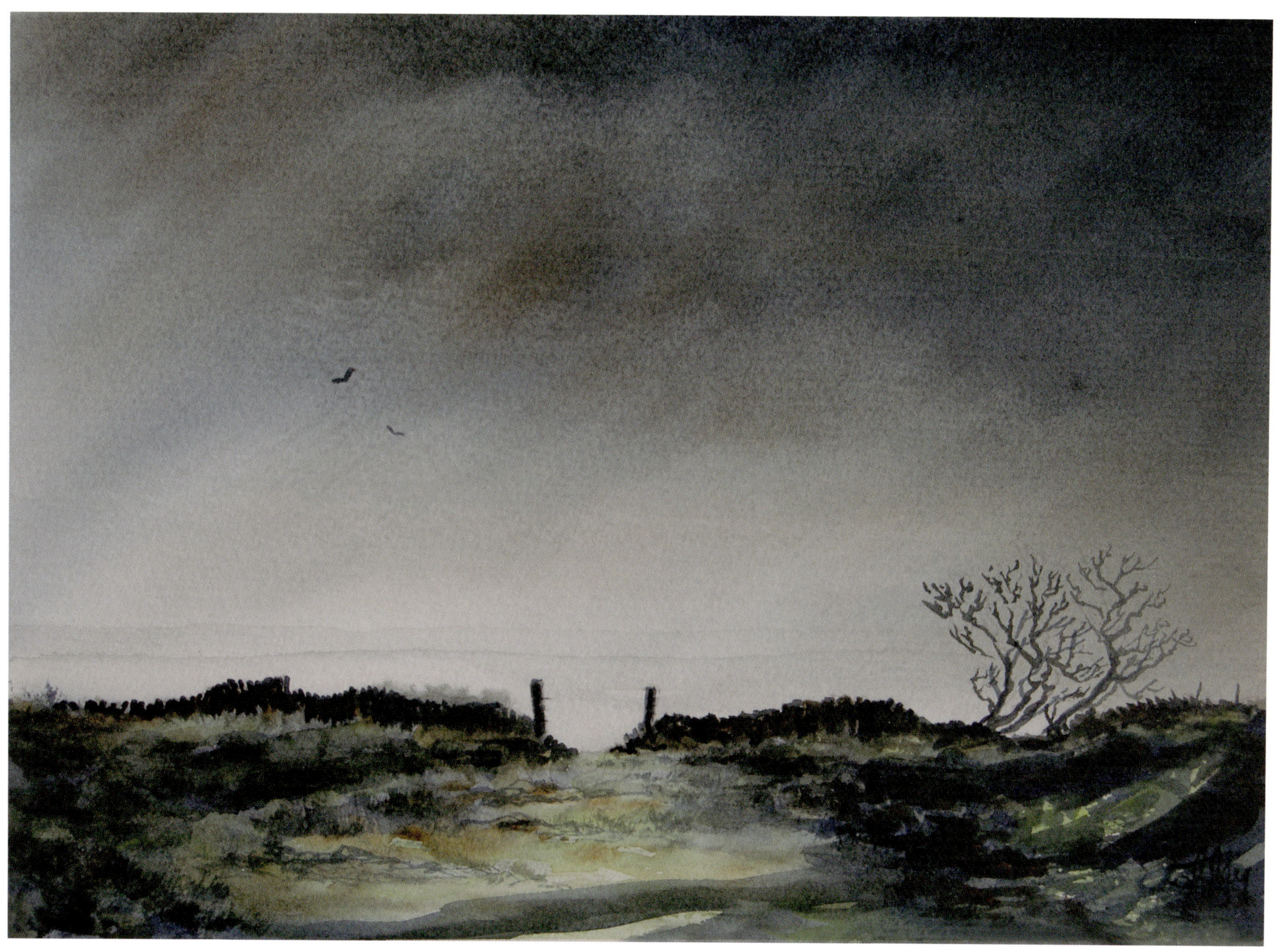

Langsett Moor, North America   91

Top Withens (Wuthering Heights)

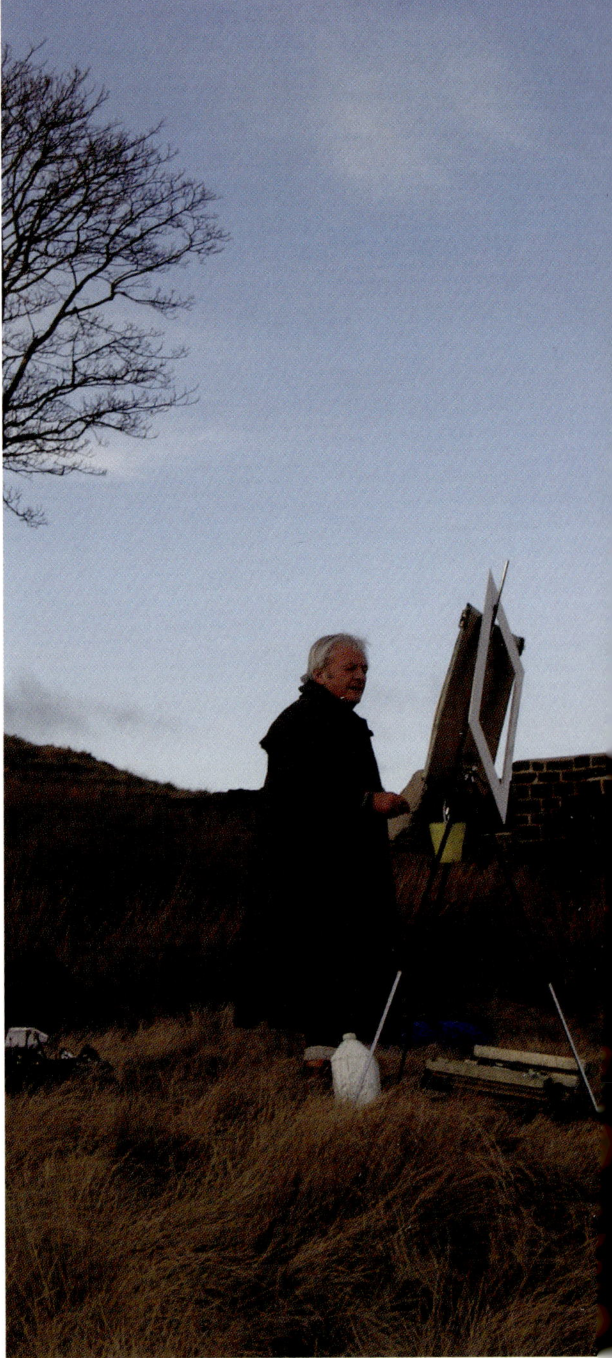

Which I first discovered in 1962, with my good friend and artist Stanley Chapman of Brighouse who is sadly no longer with us. I recently revisited it with the BBC's *Countryfile* to explain the passion I have for Yorkshire and trying to capture her moods in my paintings, in the same way that the Brontë's captured the moorland atmosphere with their words, particularly Emily Brontë in *Wuthering Heights* for which Top Withens was her inspiration. I have always had a great admiration for the Brontë sisters and at the early age of 16, I had written in my diaries: 'That what the Brontë's did with the pen, I would like to achieve with the brush.'

The moorland truly connects us, for we both try to capture a visual image and atmosphere, when someone views your painting or reads a descriptive passage you are attempting to make them feel, see and hear what you did in that one moment in time, alone on the moor.

I have always said that I am not a Barbara Cartland man, romanticising the landscape, but a Brontë man capturing the raw brooding moorland . . . it's not for everyone but it is what inspires me to paint.

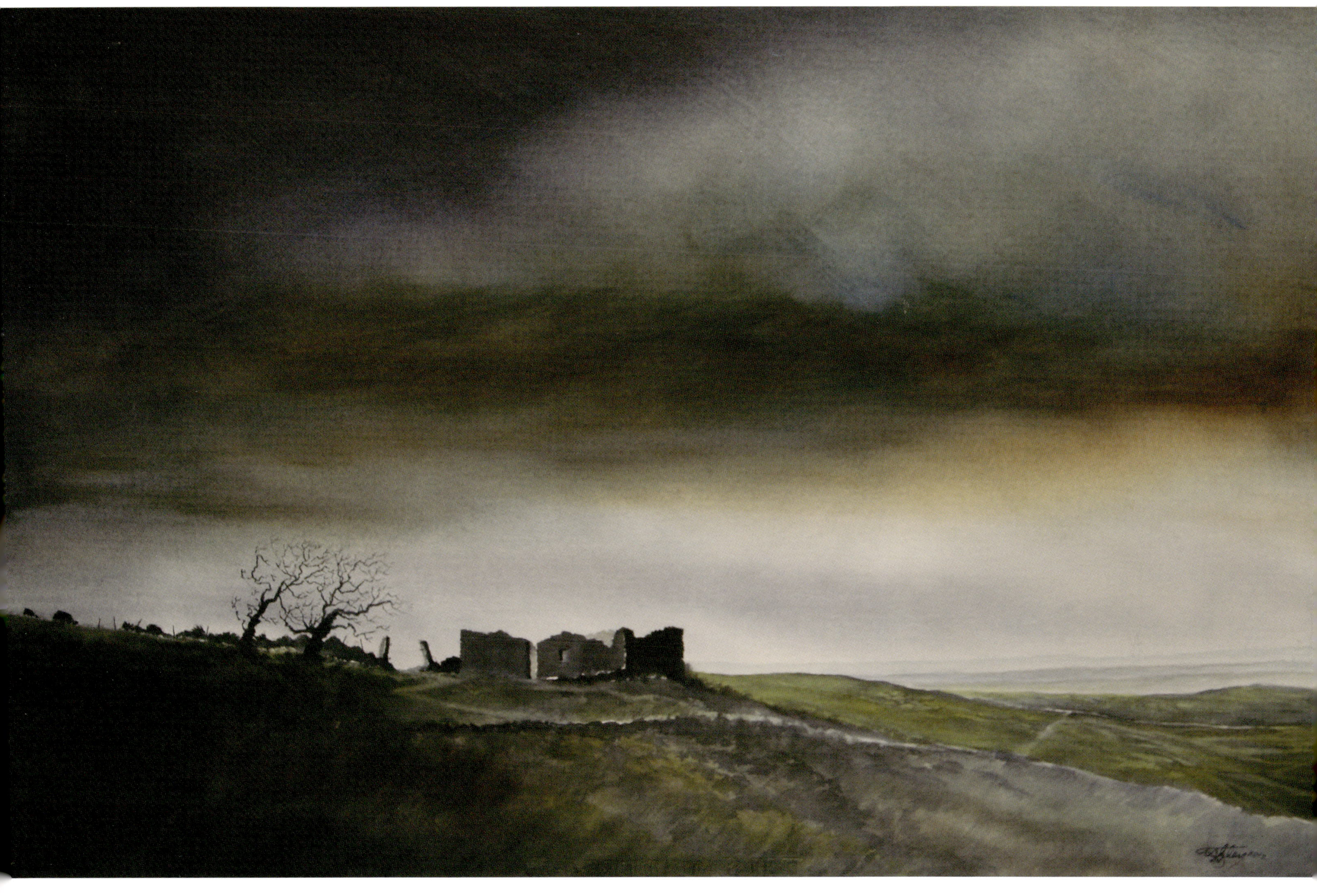

Top Withens (Wuthering Heights)   93

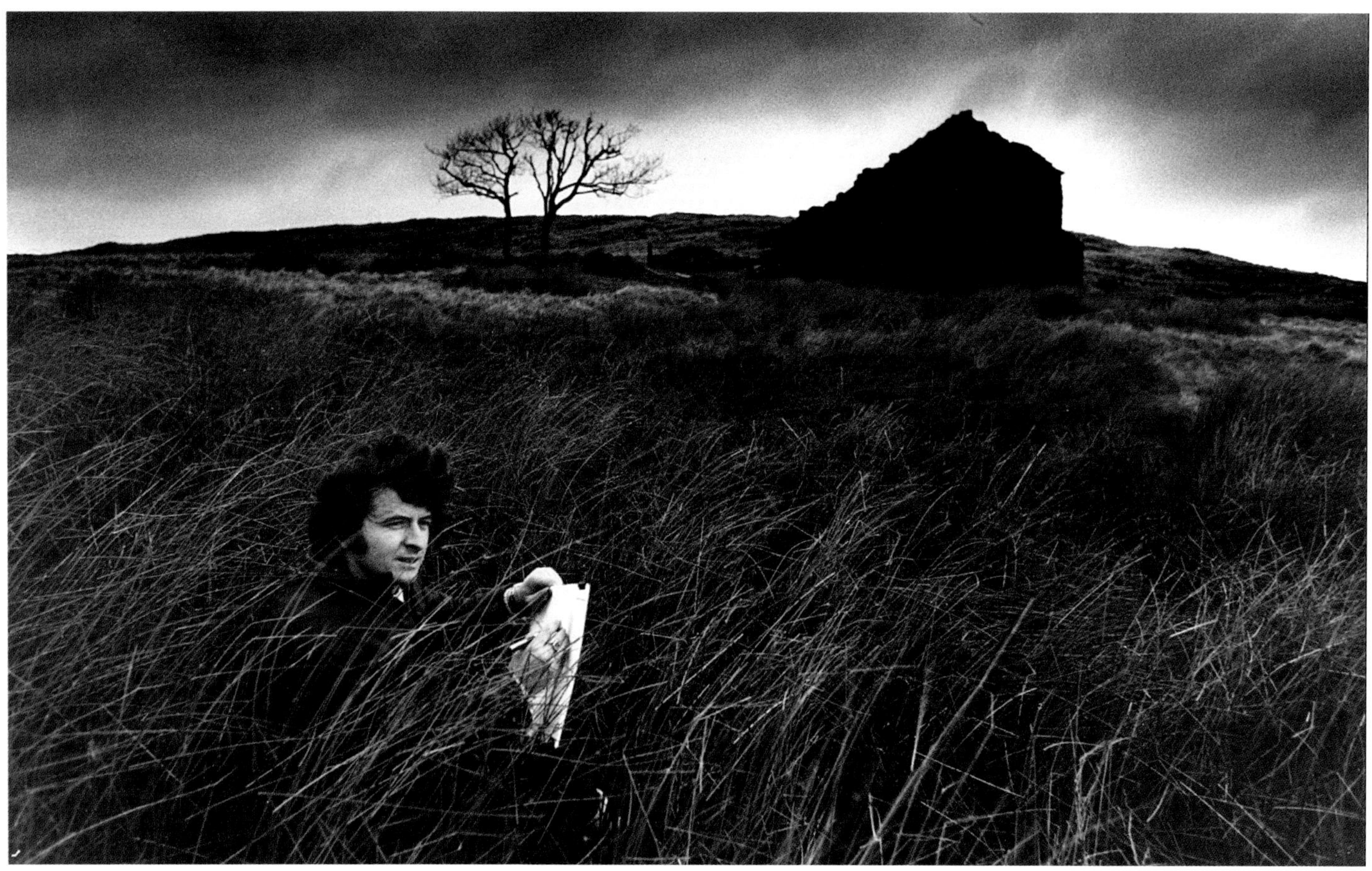

Wuthering Heights

This is how the farm at Top Withens originally stood proud on the moor. Now revisit the ruin on the previous page, for they are one and the same. Age not only diminishes our human body but also our man-made memorials until there is nothing to remember us by. The exposed landscape is notorious for its fierce wind, hence the name Withens, meaning wind.

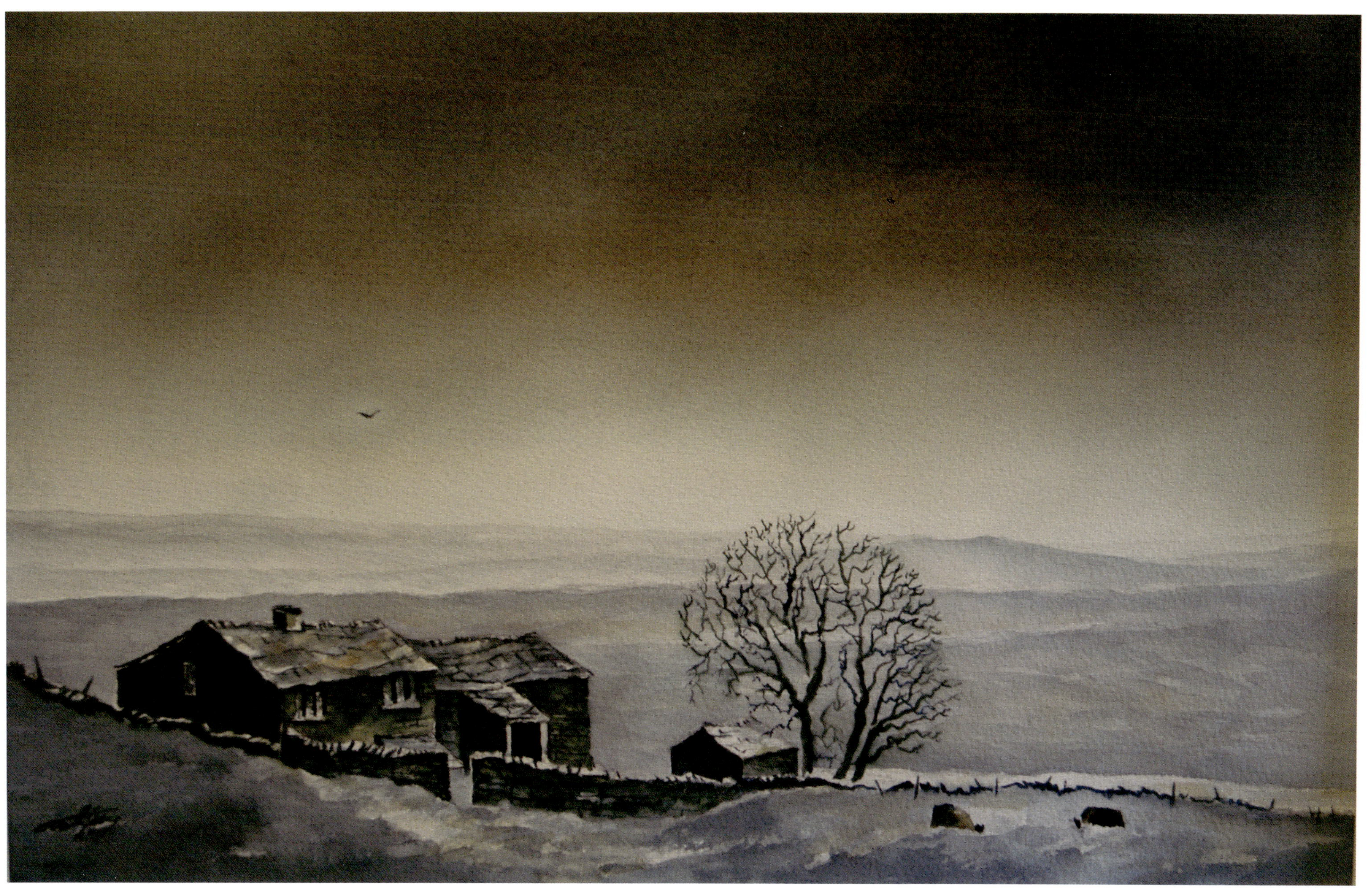

Out of the Darkness and into the Light

I have always looked for the light in the landscape for it gives you hope and colour, sharpening the painting, light takes you into the painting. Here the dark passing storm casts its shadow over the wall and across the landscape.

I find hope in the darkest of days,
and focus in the brightest.
I do not judge the universe.
(The Dalai Lama**)**

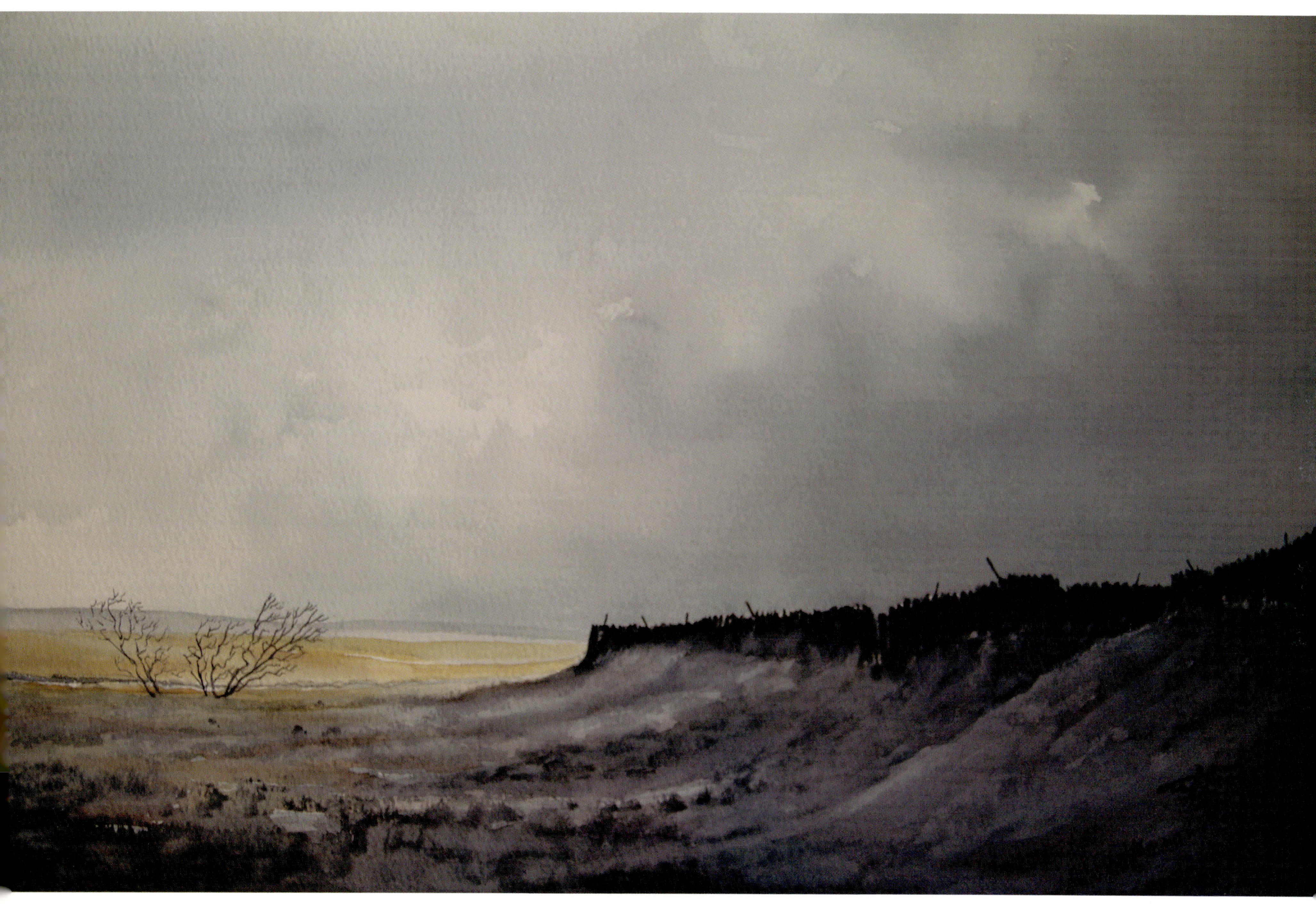

Little Blakey Howe

The Lyke Wake Walk, which I did when I was 22 with a group of friends from Barnsley. To be a dirger you had to achieve 40 miles over the open moor with just a map and compass within 24 hours as the bird flies. This part of the moorland was measured by the bird's flight. No matter how dark the day is, there is always a break of heavenly light which gives me faith.

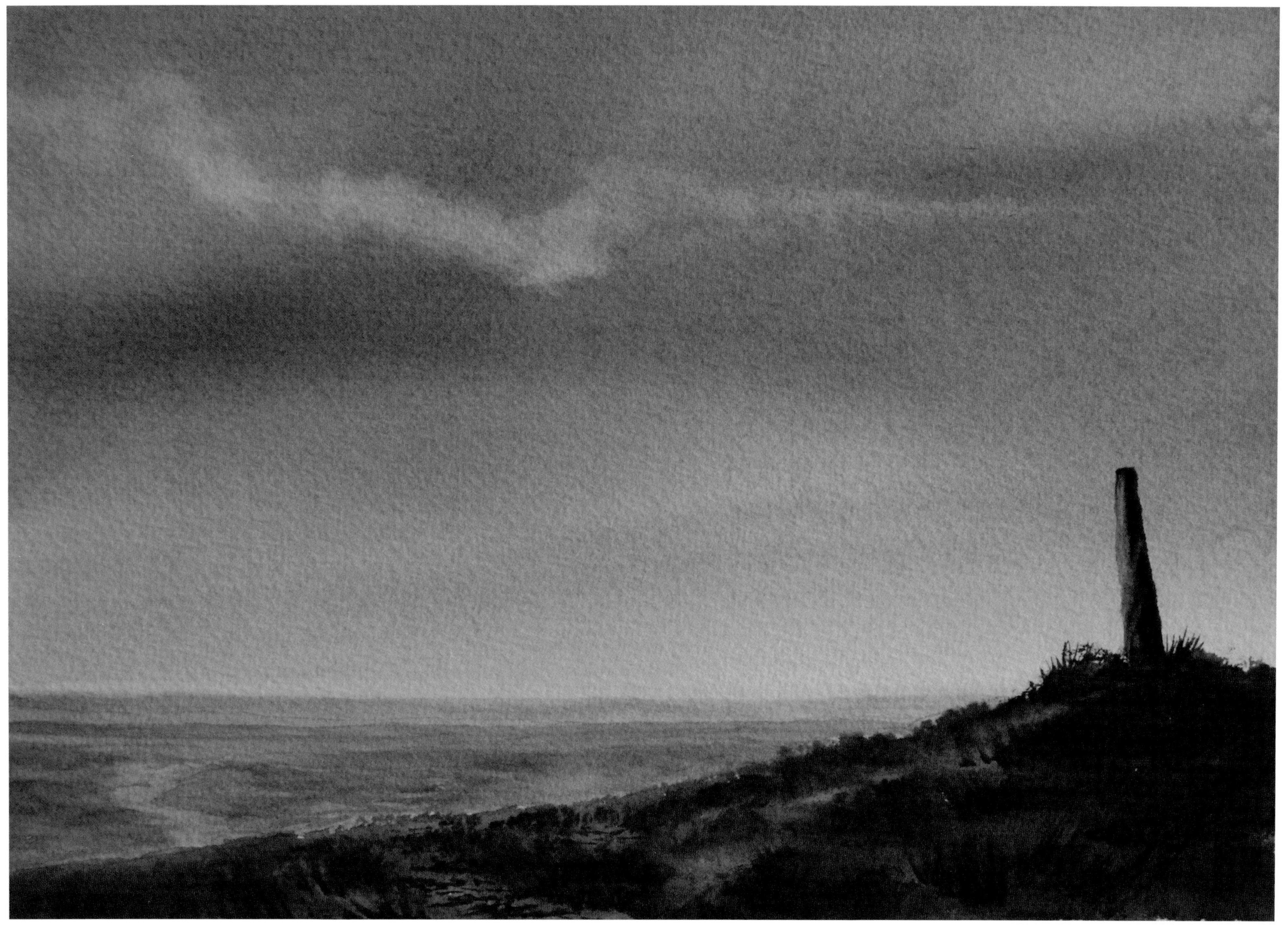

Sunlight and Shadows – Pateley Bridge

Life is very much about sunlight and shadow and there is often no rational balance. All we can do is hold on to the memories of the brighter days as we walk through the shadow and know that there is light ahead for there can be no shadow without light.

Pateley Bridge is a hidden gem in the heart of Nidderdale, a designated Area of Outstanding Natural Beauty and once visited it is easy to see why.

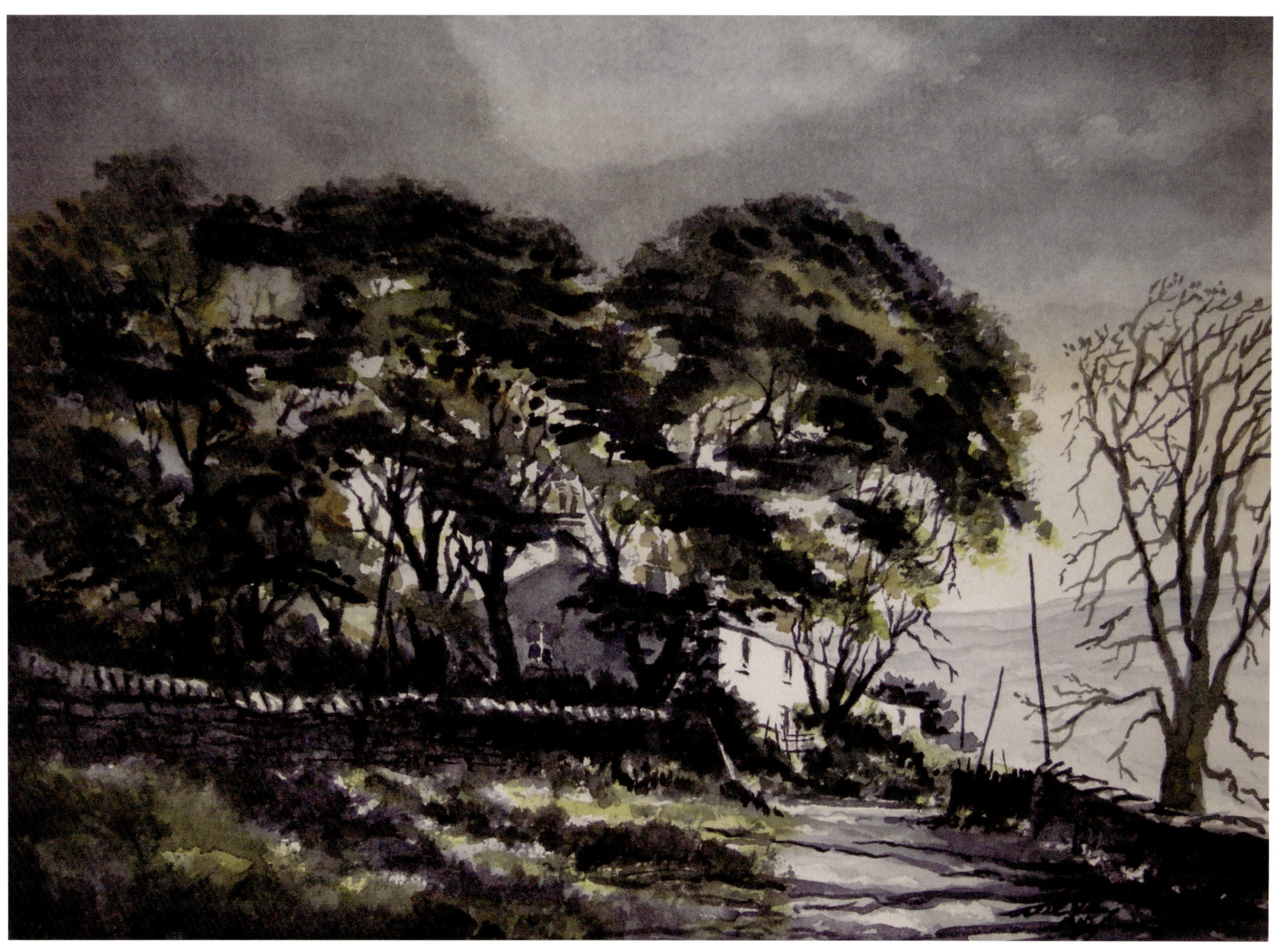

Out on its Own

The farm sits majestically on the hillside commanding the view. Even the impending storm clouds gathering do little to diminish the imposing farmhouse. Lots of farms in Yorkshire are built on hilltops: perhaps the wind dries the stone out after the storm and the higher ground avoids flooding.

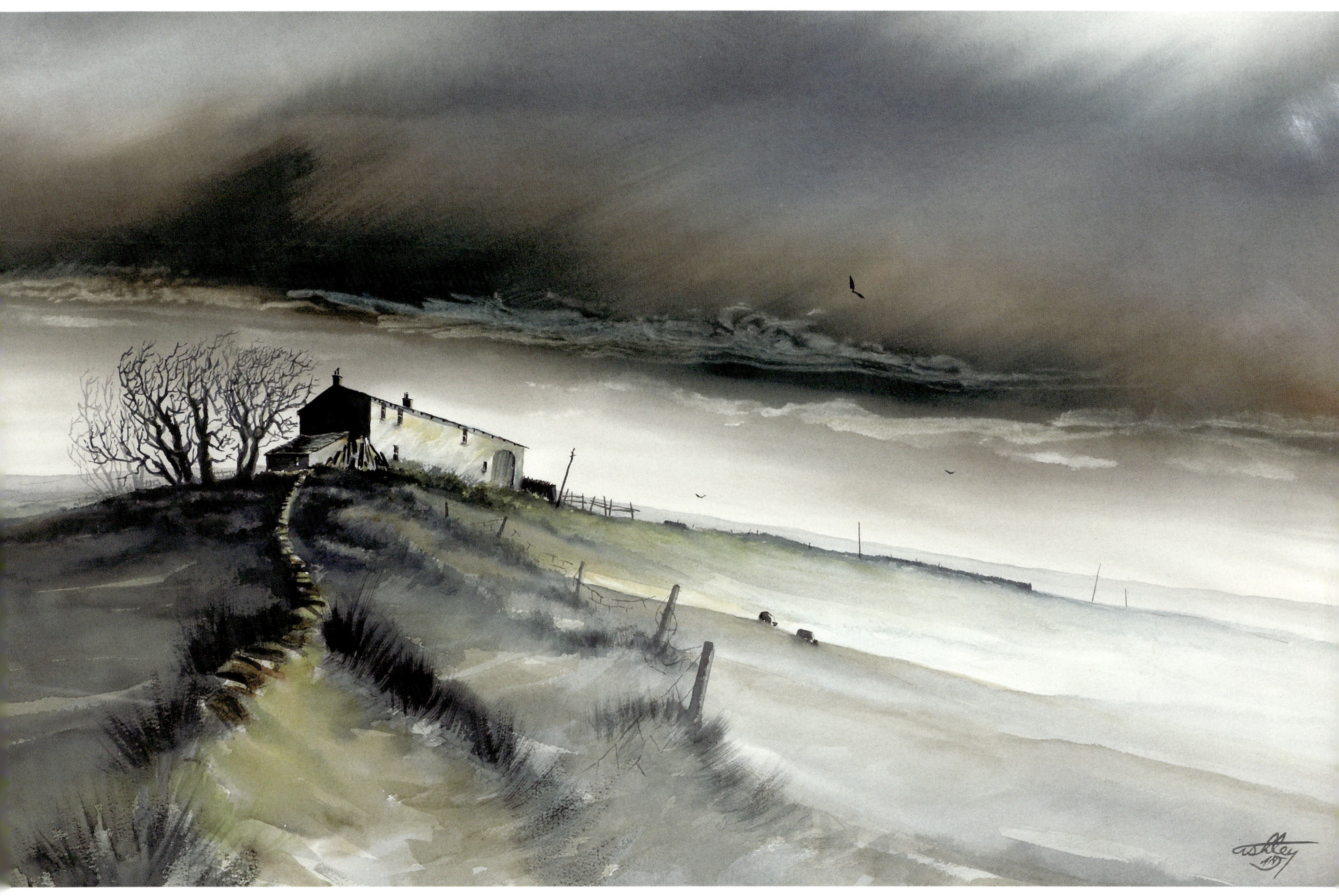

Thunderstorm approaching Rishworth Valley, Cotton Stones

The light took me into the heart of the landscape. The atmosphere of the approaching storm was such that it was as if the foreground provided the amber colour as an alert to be ready for what was to come . . . If you look closely you will see a reflection of the landscape in the sky.

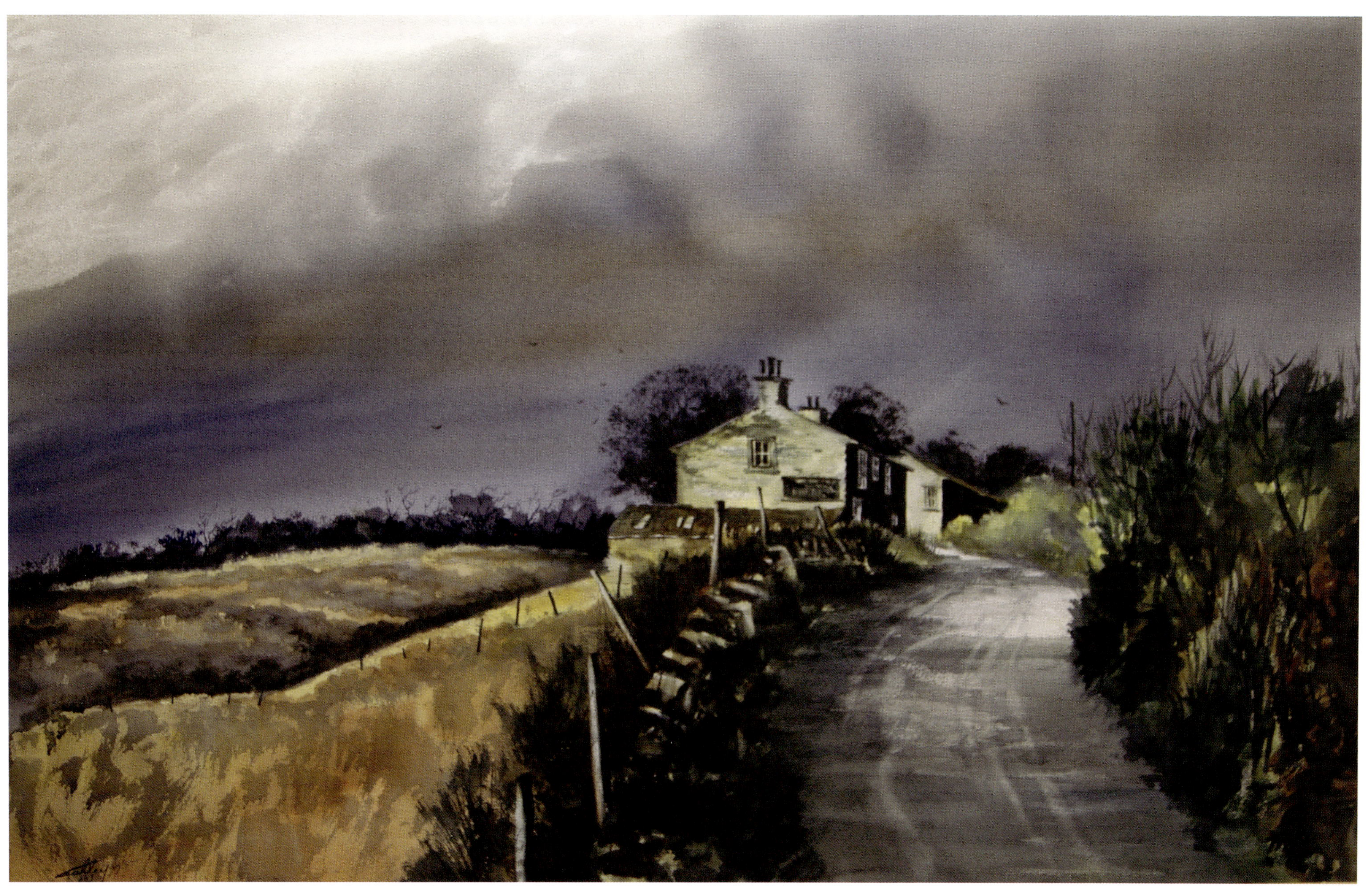

Thunderstorm approaching Rishworth Valley, Cotton Stones　　105

Muker

Winter has descended on this quiet corner of Swaledale, casting its shadows of icy blue. The farmhouse has been created expertly by someone who has knowledge of the landscape and nature, seeking refuge inside the safety of the valley with the hill for its backdrop. Keeping its inhabitants safe, you can imagine them inside, their faces glowing from the open fire whilst the weather does its worst: outside is another world away.

I always have a joke with Jon Mitchell, meteorologist for Calendar ITV, that there is no such thing as bad weather, just inappropriately dressed people, I have often seen many an untrained walker setting off in sandals or flip-flops. I find its always better to be over-prepared than under. I have had the same walking boots for many years and as an economical Yorkshireman I am sure they will see me through many more.

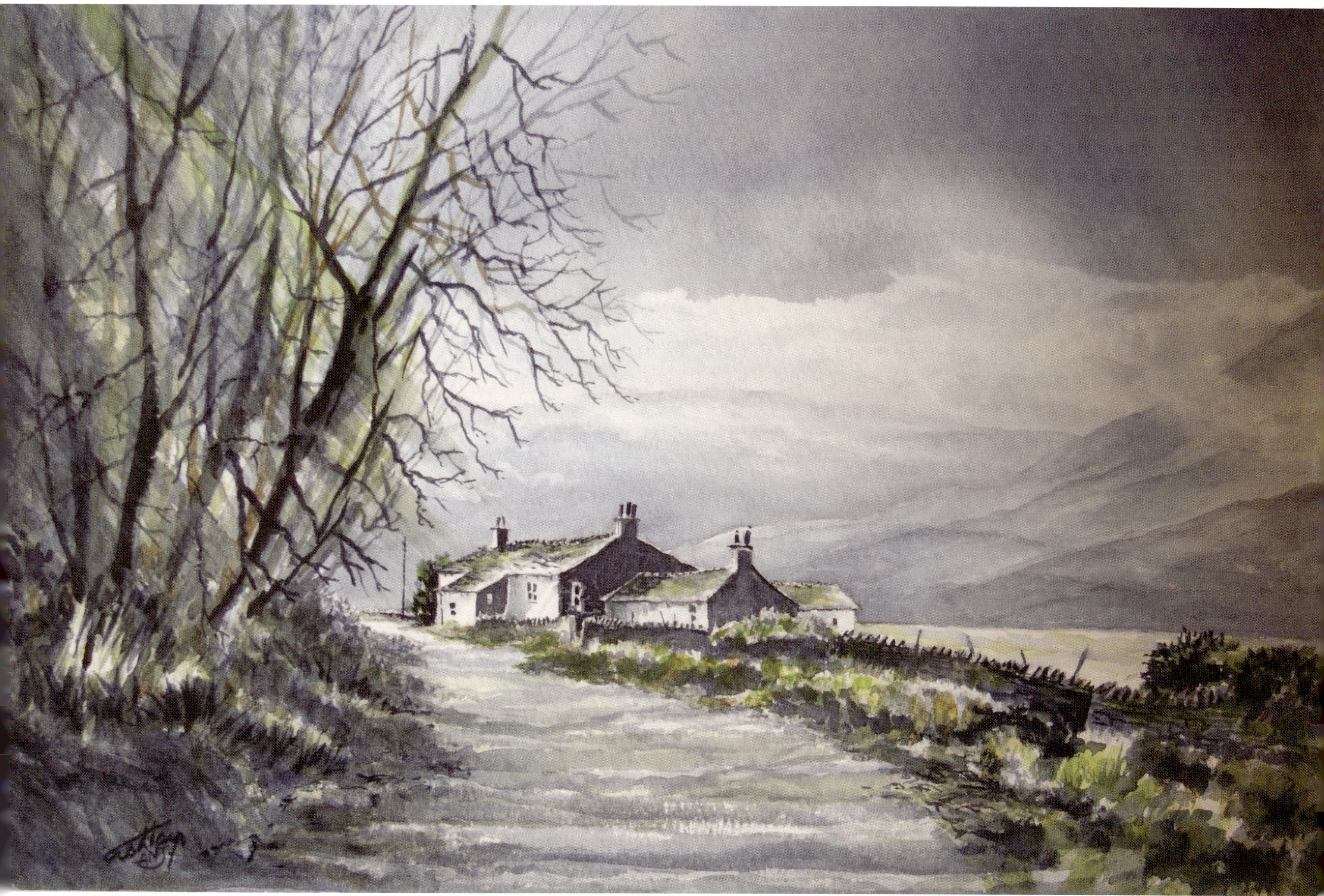

Tunnel on the Moor

The sky helps you to see the moor with ease, creating a tunnel in the sky and in the land; it speaks for itself. The tunnel takes you to its very soul and epicentre and holds you there . . . until you choose to leave.

One might ask what Yorkshire has that other landscapes do not. I would answer that not only is the landscape unique to the location but so is the weather. I know that sunshine would allow me to sell more paintings, but that is not what appeals to me. Shadows from the clouds create shapes and contour the moor land whereas sunshine flattens the light, losing the depth to the surrounding environment. Yes, rain restricts your market, but I wish to paint paintings and not pictures. To do this I need to remain true to myself and paint from my soul, enabling me to capture the passion and the atmosphere.

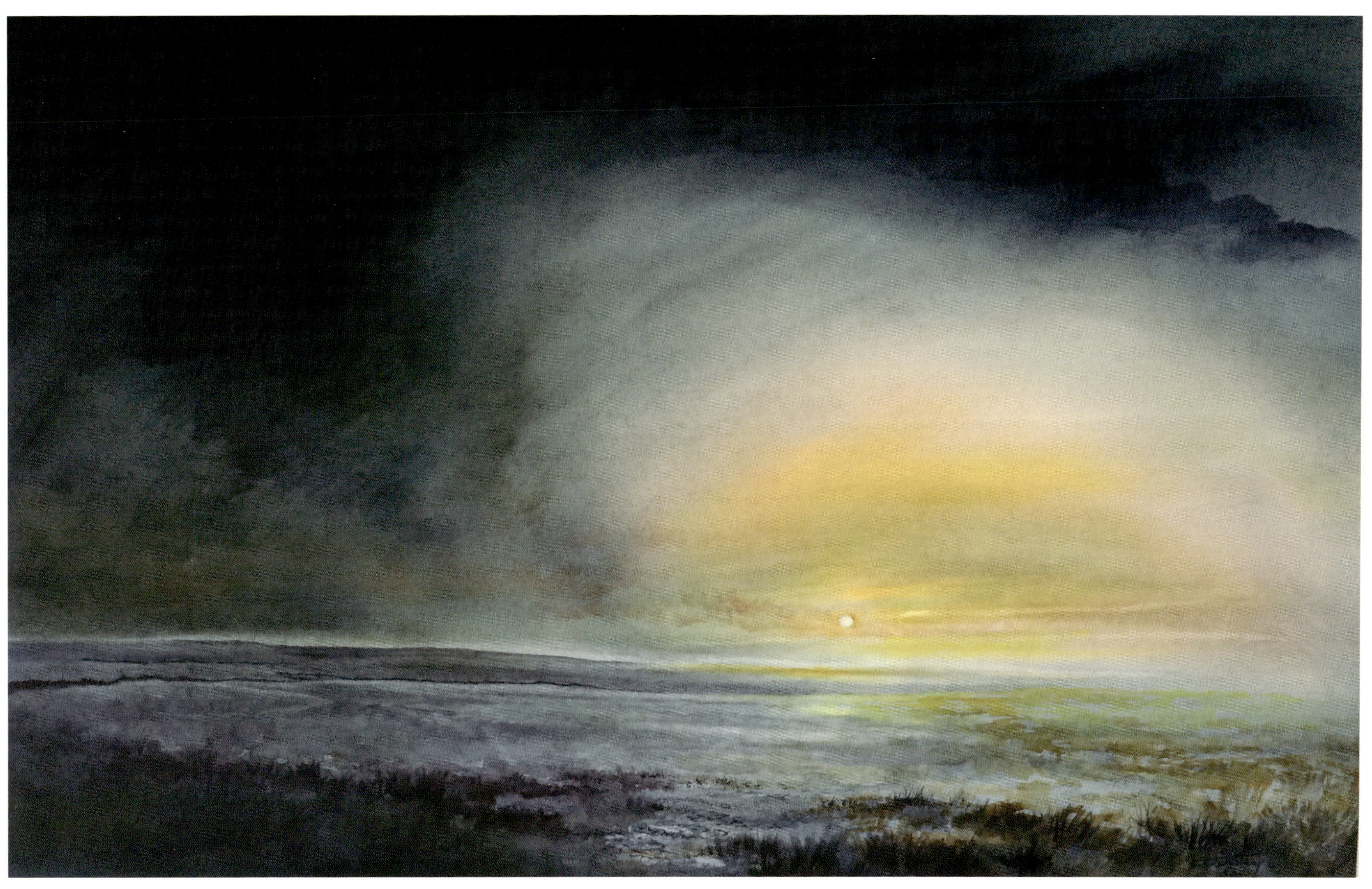

Waiting for You – Going from Nidderdale to Grassington

The farmhouse fires are lit and await the homecoming of its occupants at the end of the day. Although I am often alone on the moor, I am not alone in life with my constant. Anne, my wife of fifty-four years, who has been beside me throughout . .. waiting for me.

Grassington always brings a smile to my face as we would often bring the grandchildren on a day trip out, sketching with Grandpa with paper and pencil in hand. It was on such occasion that, on highlighting the danger of slippery stones around water, I proceeded to fall into a stream, ensuring that every layer of clothing was wet through. Retreating to the car, we drove to Grassington, the nearest village where upon my wife purchased new clothing at the Outward Bound shop which I changed into in the car. The grandchildren remember this to this day.

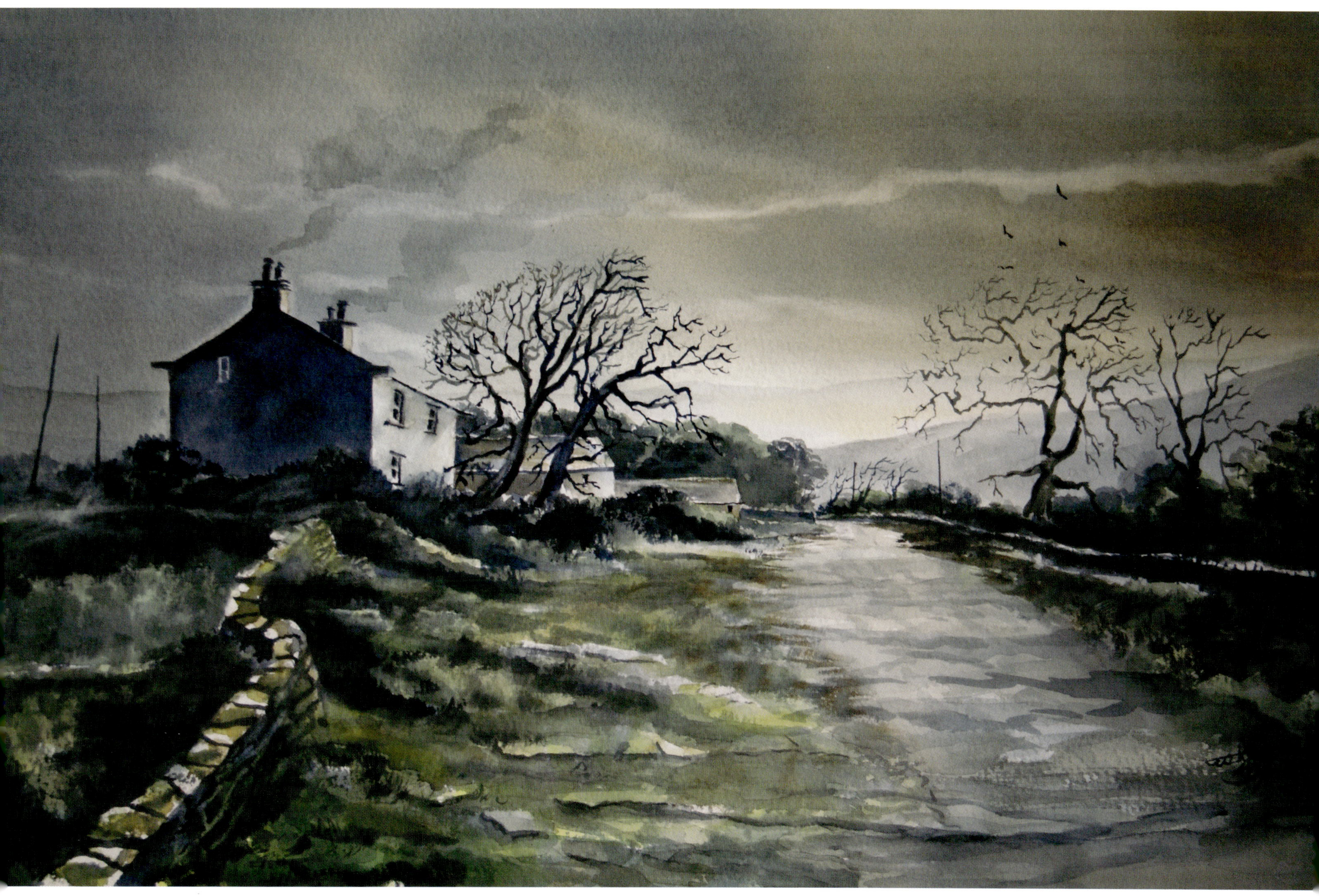

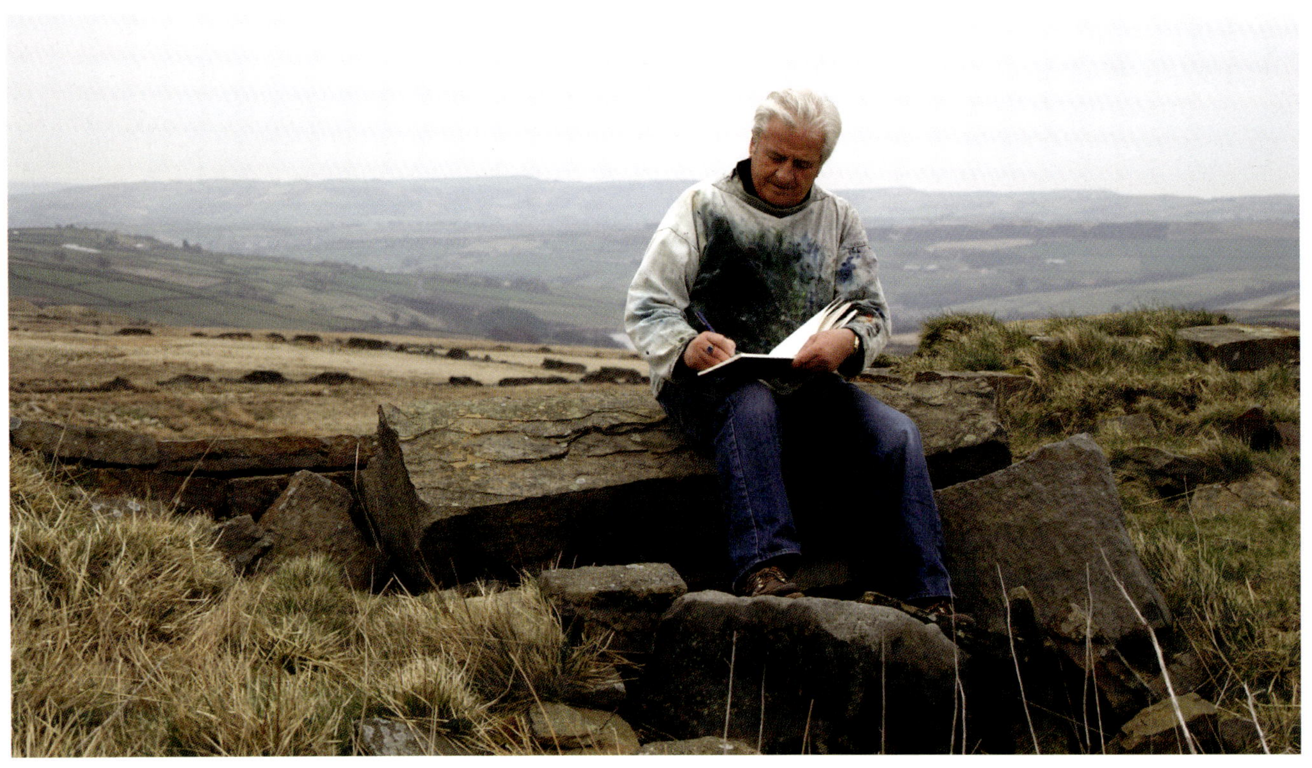

Away from it all,
'Thank God'

Just me and the sheep . . . I am not an unsociable or insular man, but when I am on the
moors I am free, free to walk, to sketch, to breathe.

I'll walk where my own nature would be leading: It vexes me to choose another guide.
(Emily Brontë)

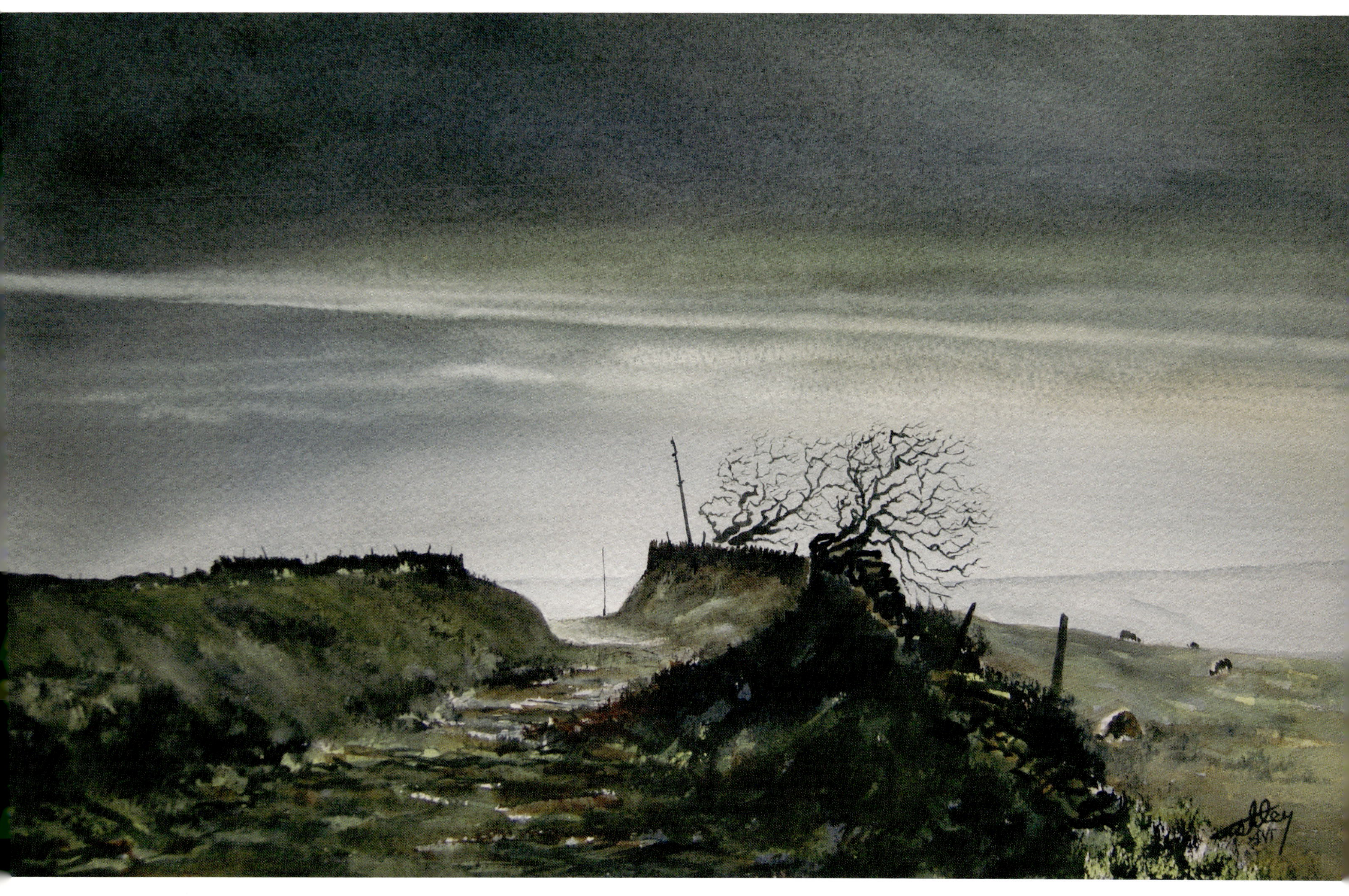

Farmhouse on Blackshaw Moor

Blackshaw is a parish in Calderdale and its moorland is a contrast to its neighbour Kirklees. Across the valley is Stoodley Pike, with a monument erected by public subscription which was commenced in 1814 to commemorate the surrender of Paris to the Allies, dominating the moors above Todmoden. Even on this bright day, smoke rises from the chimneys, showing the true temperature.

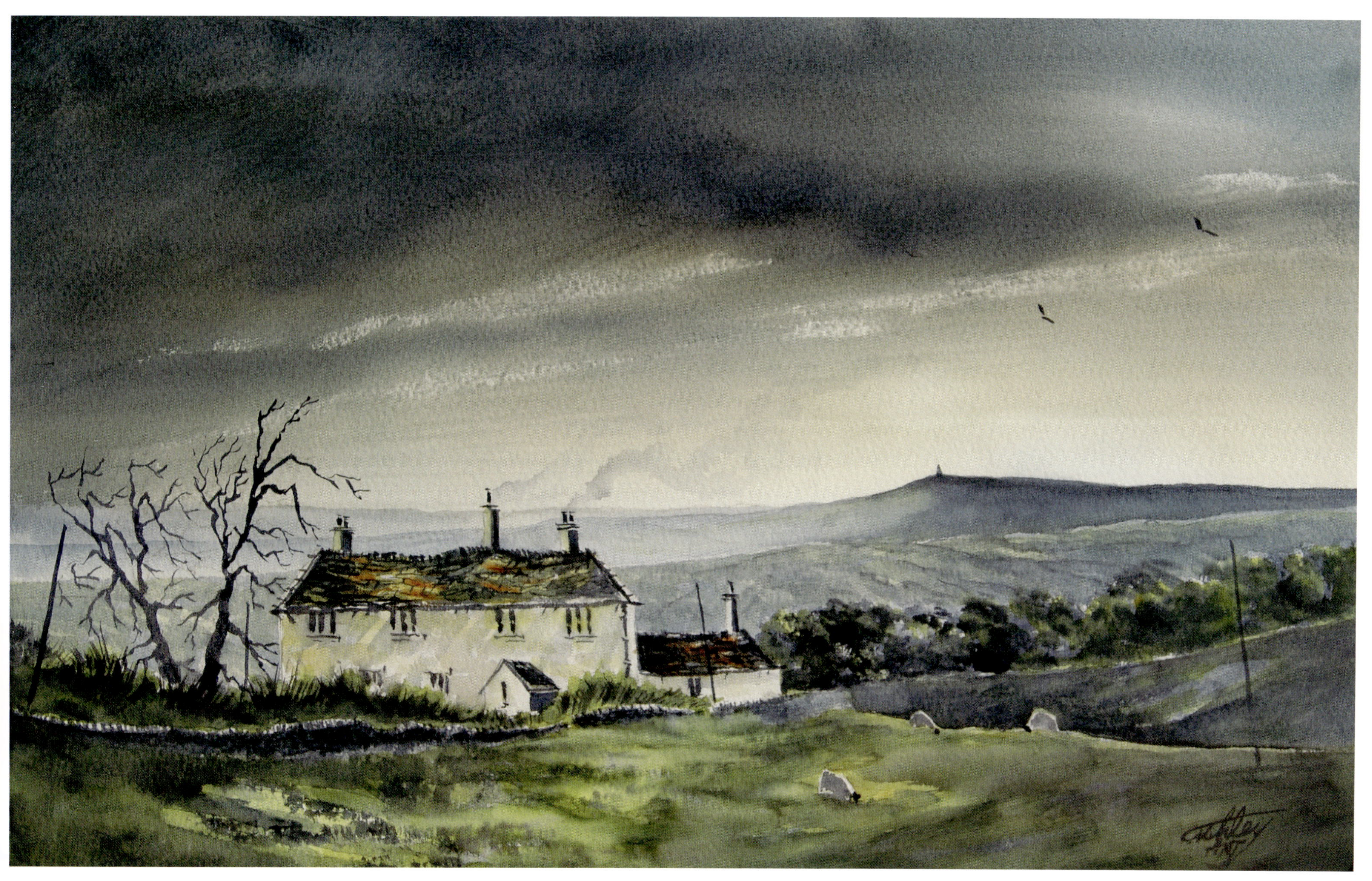

Farms on Ribblesdale Head

Even though totally exposed, the autumn sun casts its glow across the moorland, creating not only warmth but also silhouettes out of the farm and its outbuilding.

Nearby is the Ribbleshead viaduct. Made up of twenty-four arches, it carries the Settle–Carlisle Railway across the valley, created by over a thousand navvies with numerous deaths during the four years of construction. It is a stunning feature of architecture and a tribute to what man can achieve without modern equipment.

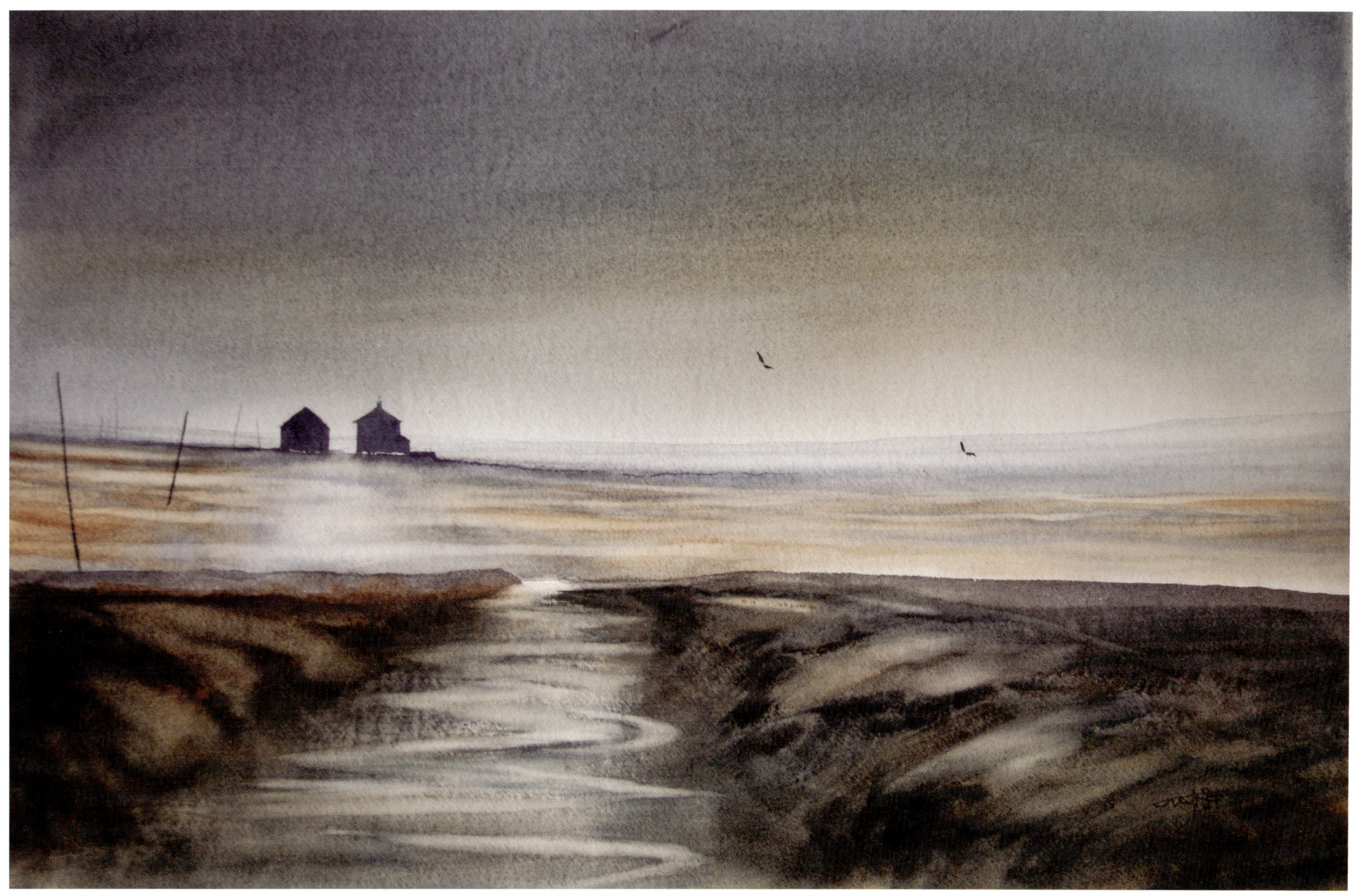

Foxup Beck

Foxup is a hamlet in the Yorkshire Dales. Would you believe the title means upstream with foxes? The source of the River Skirfare starts here. The natural contours of the valley offer the farmhouse some protection from the elements.

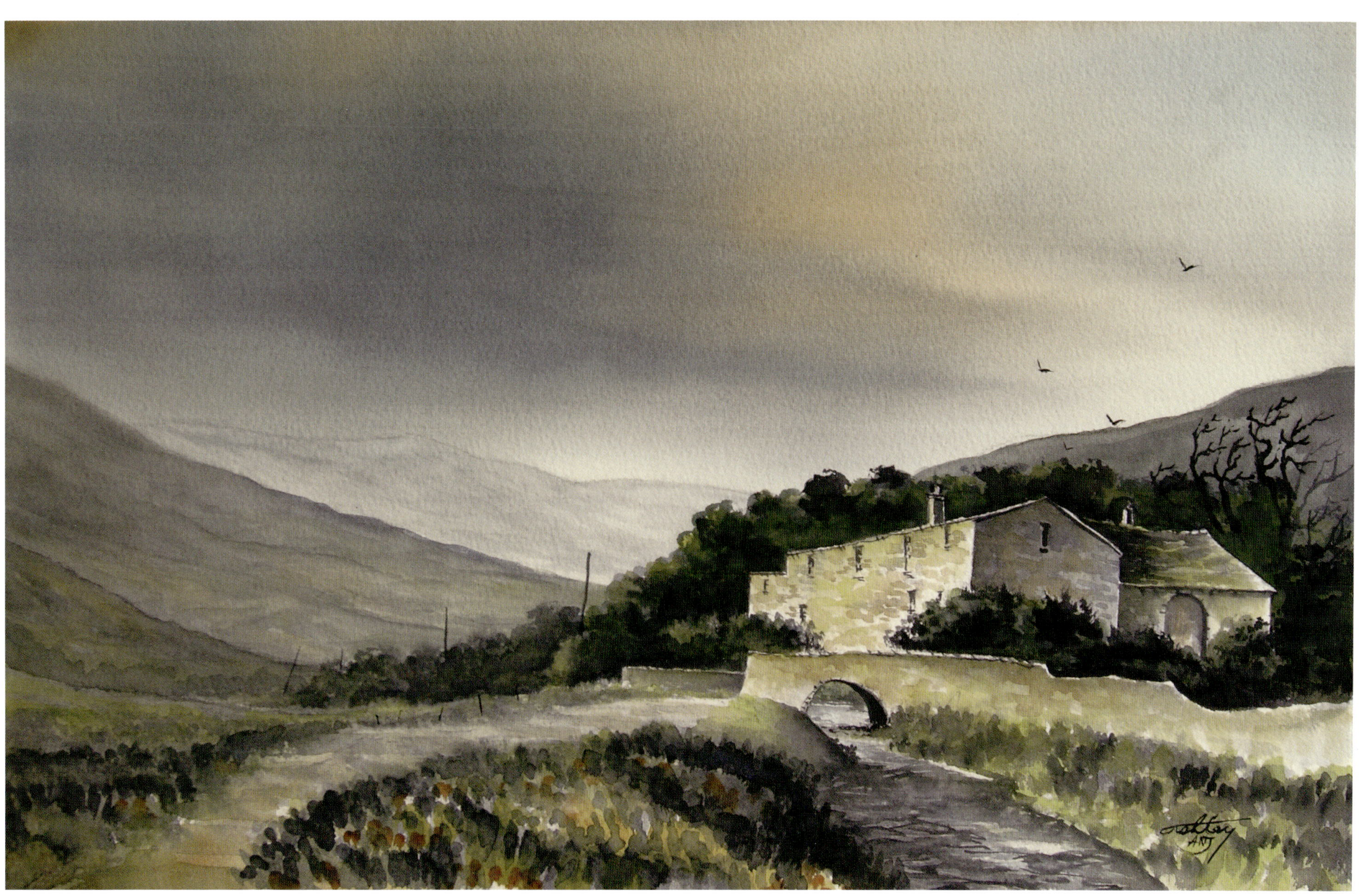

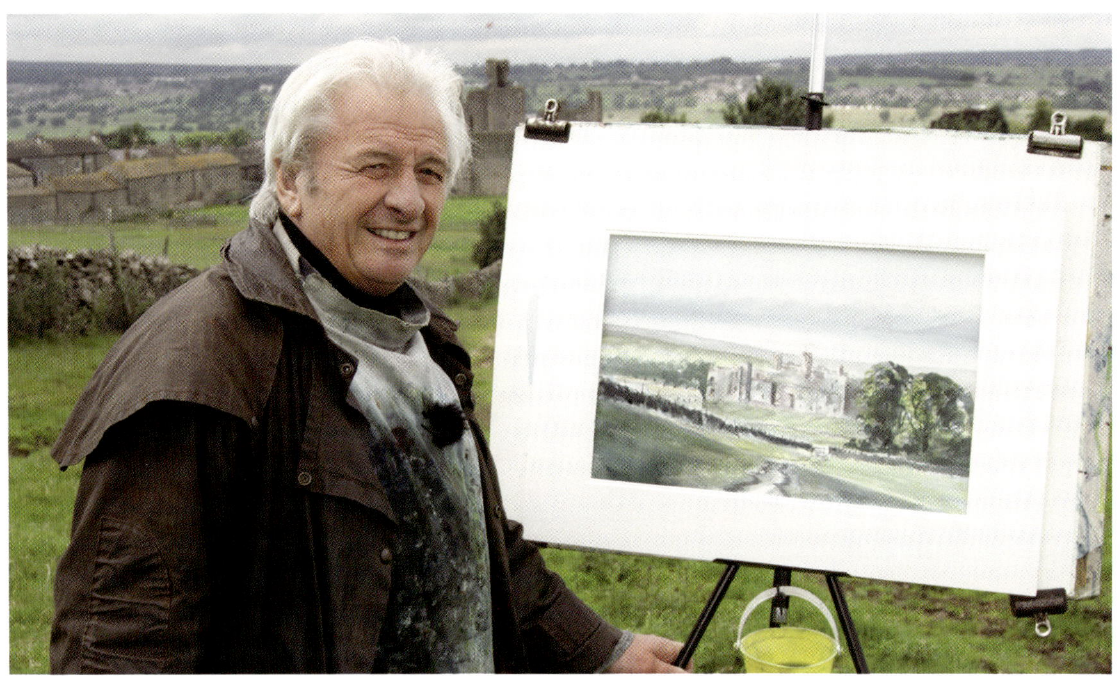

Middleham Castle

This was drawn from where J. M. W. Turner, the greatest English landscape artist, once stood and painted. He toured Yorkshire and its Dales on horseback. Middleham today has an established history of over 200 years of racehorse training and has turned out at least three Grand National winners.

It was a privilege to work with Welcome to Yorkshire on the launch of 'The Turner Trail', an interactive map that allows you to locate numerous locations (seventy-six) throughout Yorkshire which the great British landscape watercolour artist visited on his tours of the county. He visited Middleham Castle on his Yorkshire Grand Tour of 1816 and, looking at the number of sketches he produced, was inspired by the vista. As the renowned 'Painter of Light', Turner has always been my inspiration but I do not wish to emulate his work, though through studying his work I can gain an insight in to his use of light and shade.

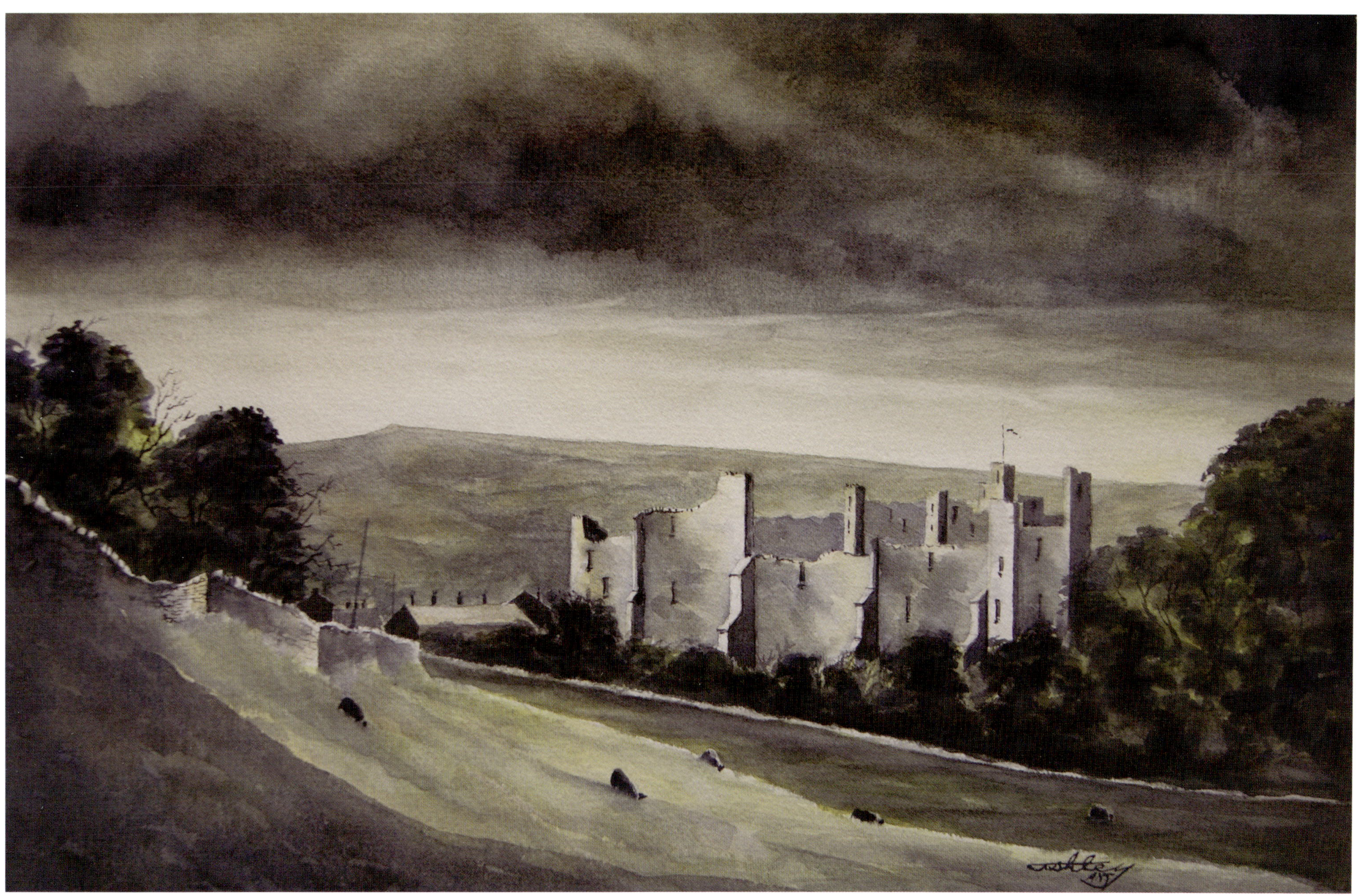

Mist and Low Cloud, Wensleydale

A fact that non-walkers may not know is that Wensleydale is the only Dale not named by the river as the river passing through its valley is called the Ure. The likes of Wharfedale and Swaledale are all named after their rivers. Here the mist has descended but yet the blue of the receding uplands are still visible as they push back into the distance.

It was once again raining but as I always say 'Better to be alive on a rainy day than dead on a sunny day': my family have come to understand my dark sense of humour.

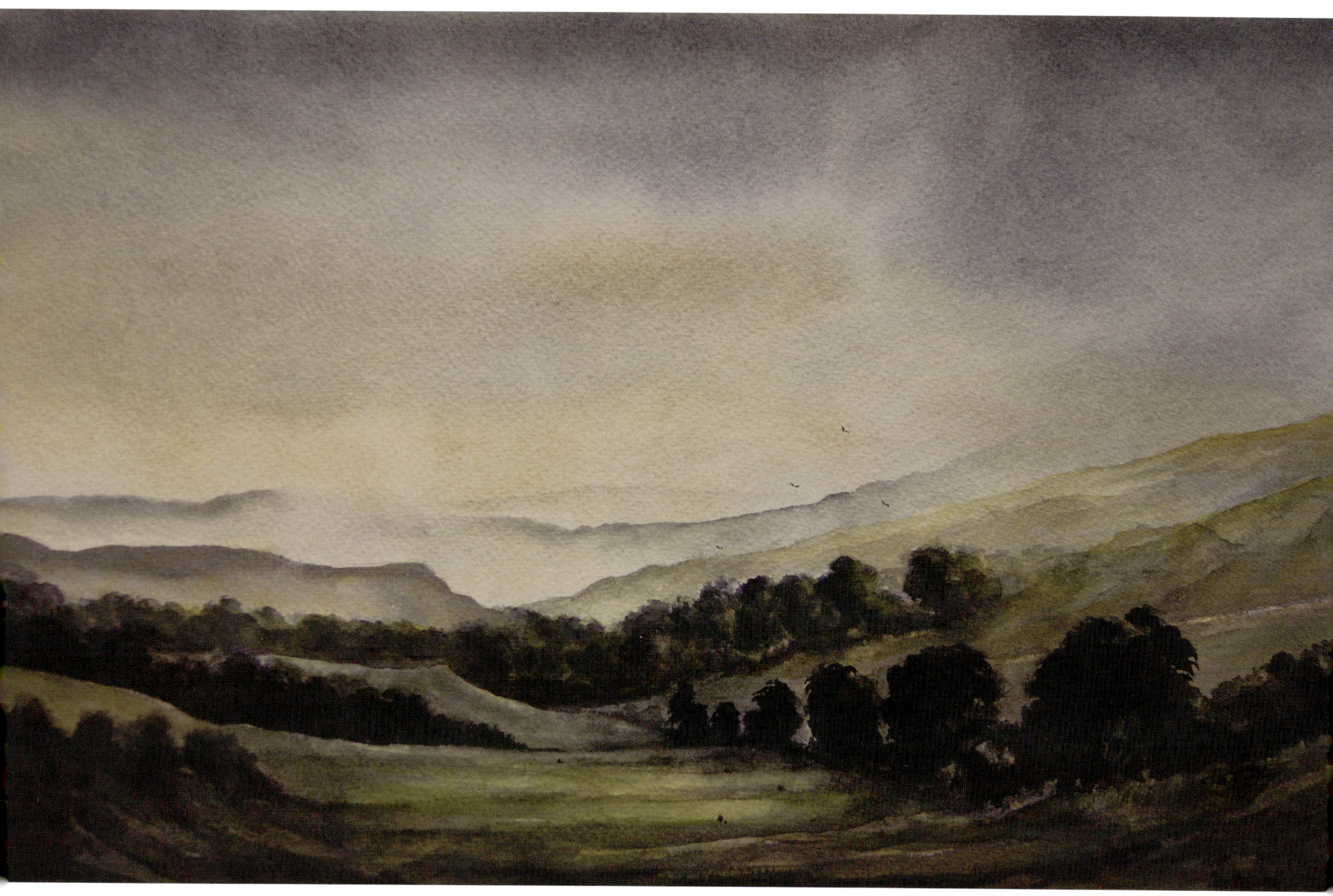

Strines Moor near Langsett

Like a mosaic, the stones have been laid by others to ensure that walkers keep to the path and prevent destruction of the landscape. In our quest to enjoy the moorland it is important to also be respectful, for where we lead others will follow and vegetation is destroyed as we create new paths across the landscape. On this day there was such a contrast of colour, the purple heather, the almost luminous green of the bilberry bushes and the Prussian-blue sky leaving light where it met the horizon. You have to be quick to pick the bilberries for sheep are prolific munchers given the chance.

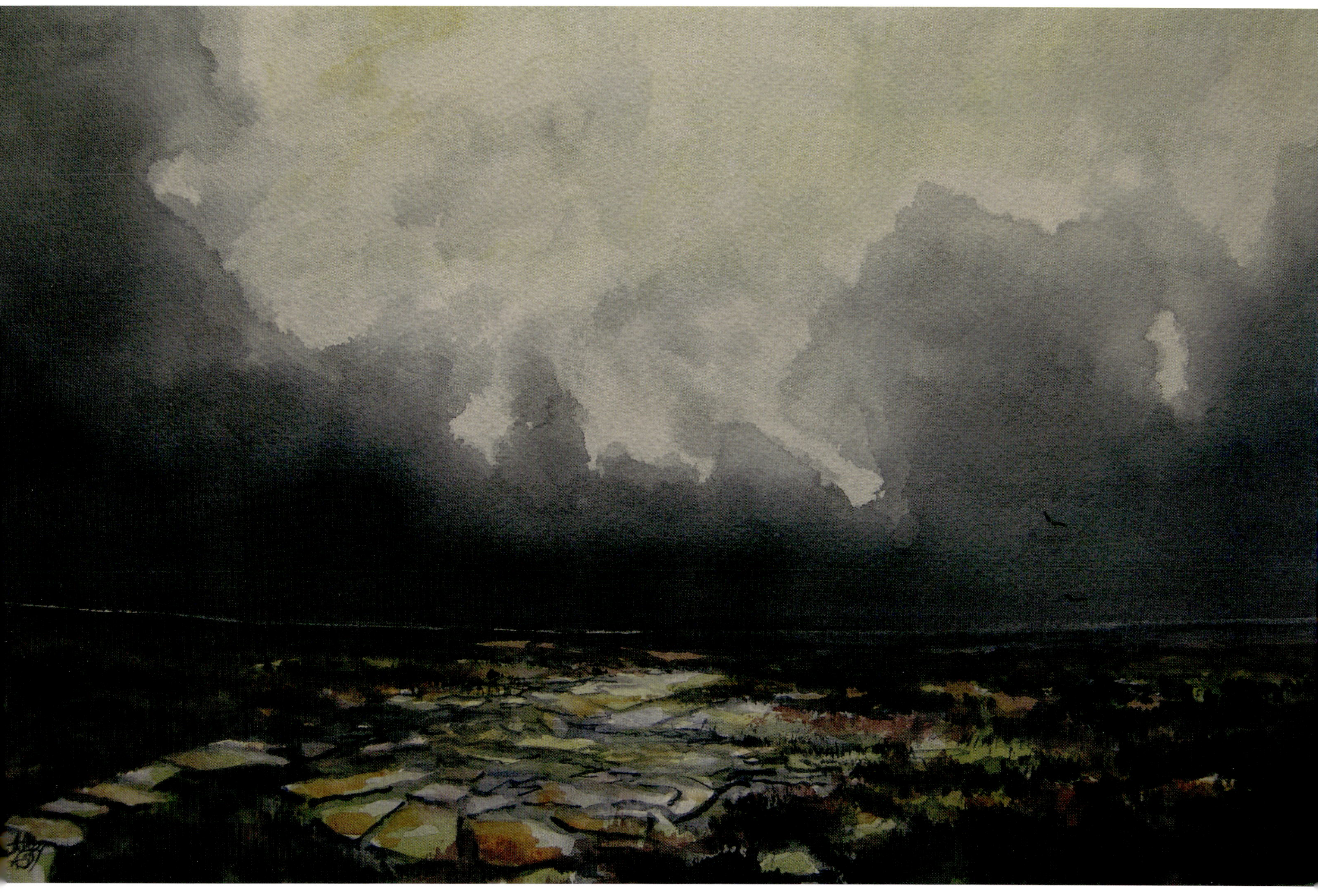

The Farm – Tan Hill to Reeth

The farm appears to be a tranquil location on this summer's day. At first glance you could be forgiven for wishing to be away from it all with the soft colours of the landscape and the sheep grazing nearby in the field, it looks idyllic. Then look again, more closely and you will see the direction of the trees, all forced to grow in one direction by the strong prevailing winds, for this is the landscape from Tan Hill to Reeth, where Britain's highest public house is situated and a small drop of whisky is truly medicinal.

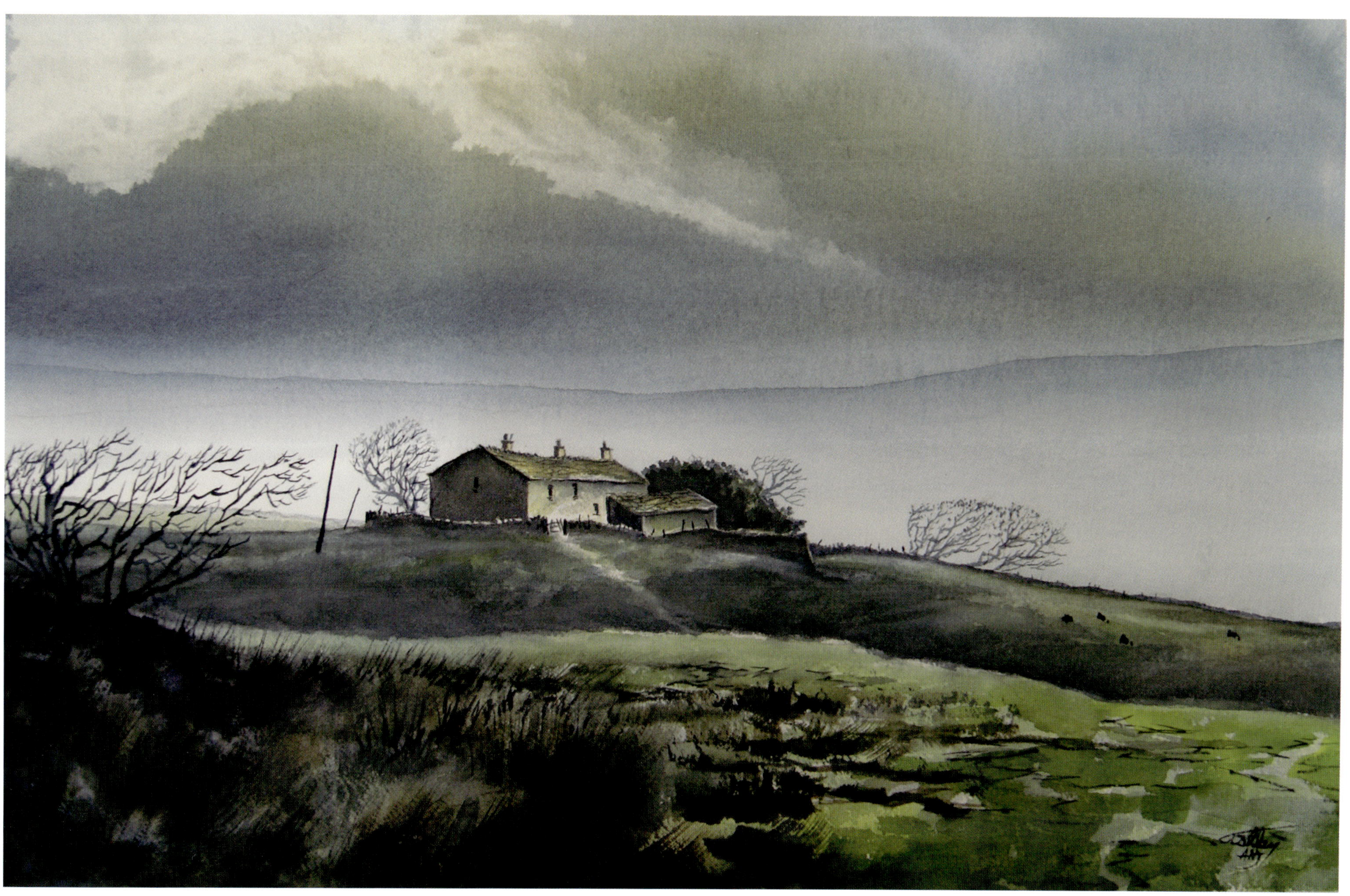

The Pennine Moor, Wessenden

Wessenden, Marsden Moor, is more than a location to me, it has been my moral compass, from moving my young family here, opening a gallery in the valley and living my life. The moor has always been at my side. I call it my 'Love Affair' with the moors, for this is what it means to me.

I am proud that 'Framing the Landscape' launched with its very first frame at Wessenden, for I wish to share my passion for this great landscape: it is not mine alone but for everyone to enjoy. My one wish is that others will explore and view the ever-changing landscape, as Mother Nature has given us the gift of a fantastic exhibition; we just need to make time to stop and appreciate what is before us. The free-standing metal frame is intended to focus our vision to frame the landscape.

It is with mutual respect that the National Trust has become a partner in 'Framing the Landscape' for we share the same passion and protection for a landscape that is our children's heritage.

The University of Huddersfield has been influential in the creation of the free-standing easels assisting with the design of the frame, prototype and construction of the full-scale frames; their assistance in this has been invaluable. Thanks also must go to sponsors and partners; The National Trust, Walker Morris and Grand Central Rail.

The landscape is more than just a view, and with 'Framing the Landscape' I hope that others will see it as I do using all your senses to engage, to feel the rain on your face, to smell the bracken, to hear the skylark and to value all these simple pleasures.

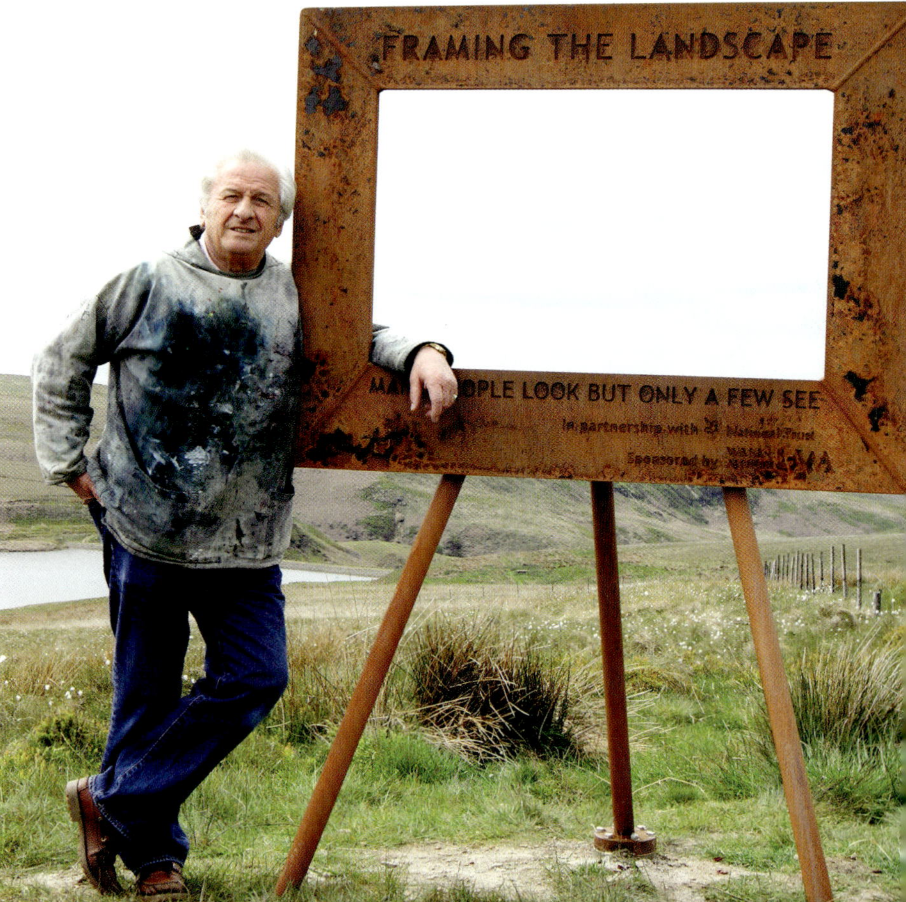

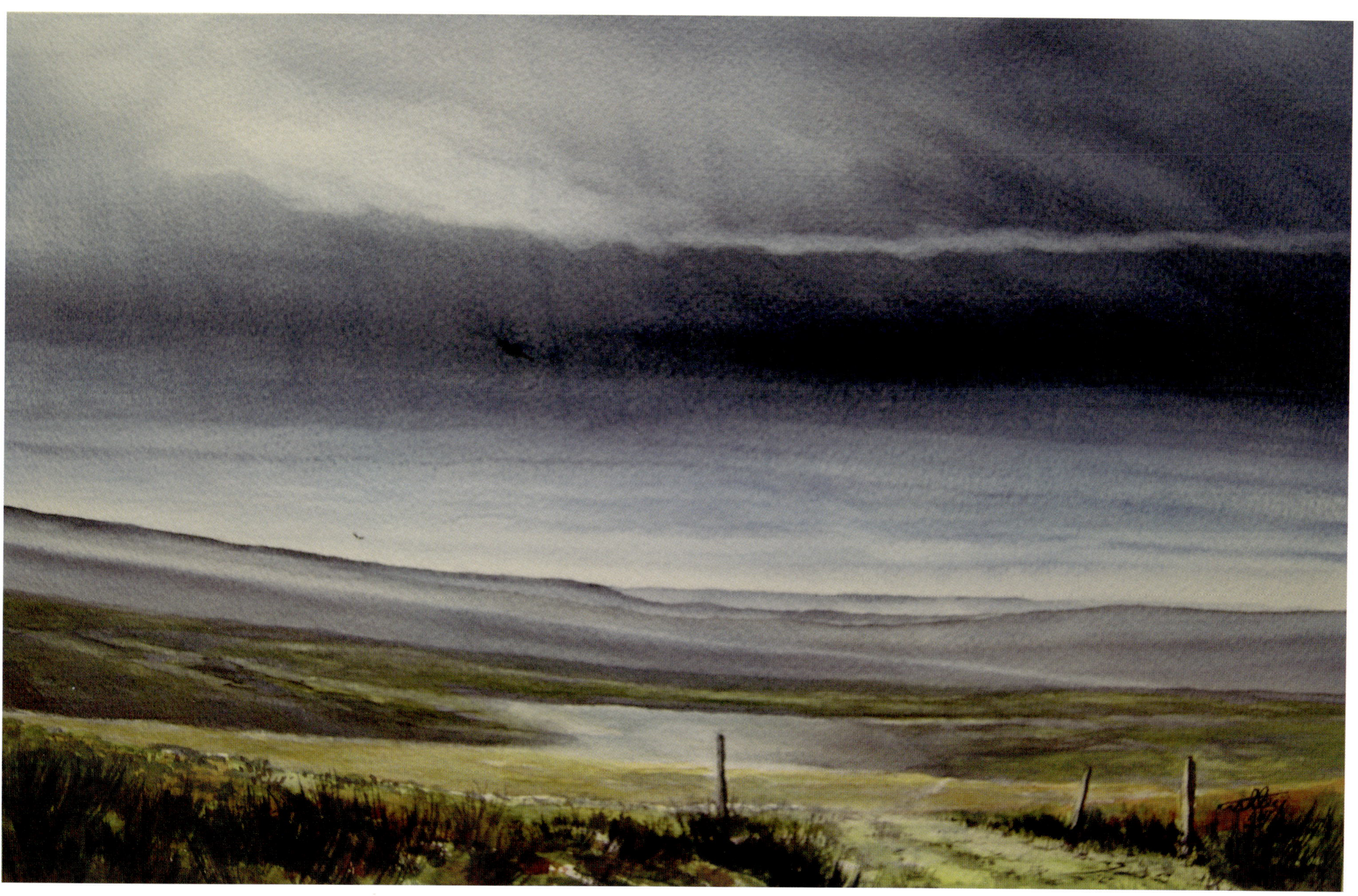

Westerdale

Within the Scarborough district of North Yorkshire, the road ahead created a feeling of light, not only in light and shade but in mood. It felt like the day was waiting to be filled, like a white crisp page ready to be written on, giving hope to each new day.

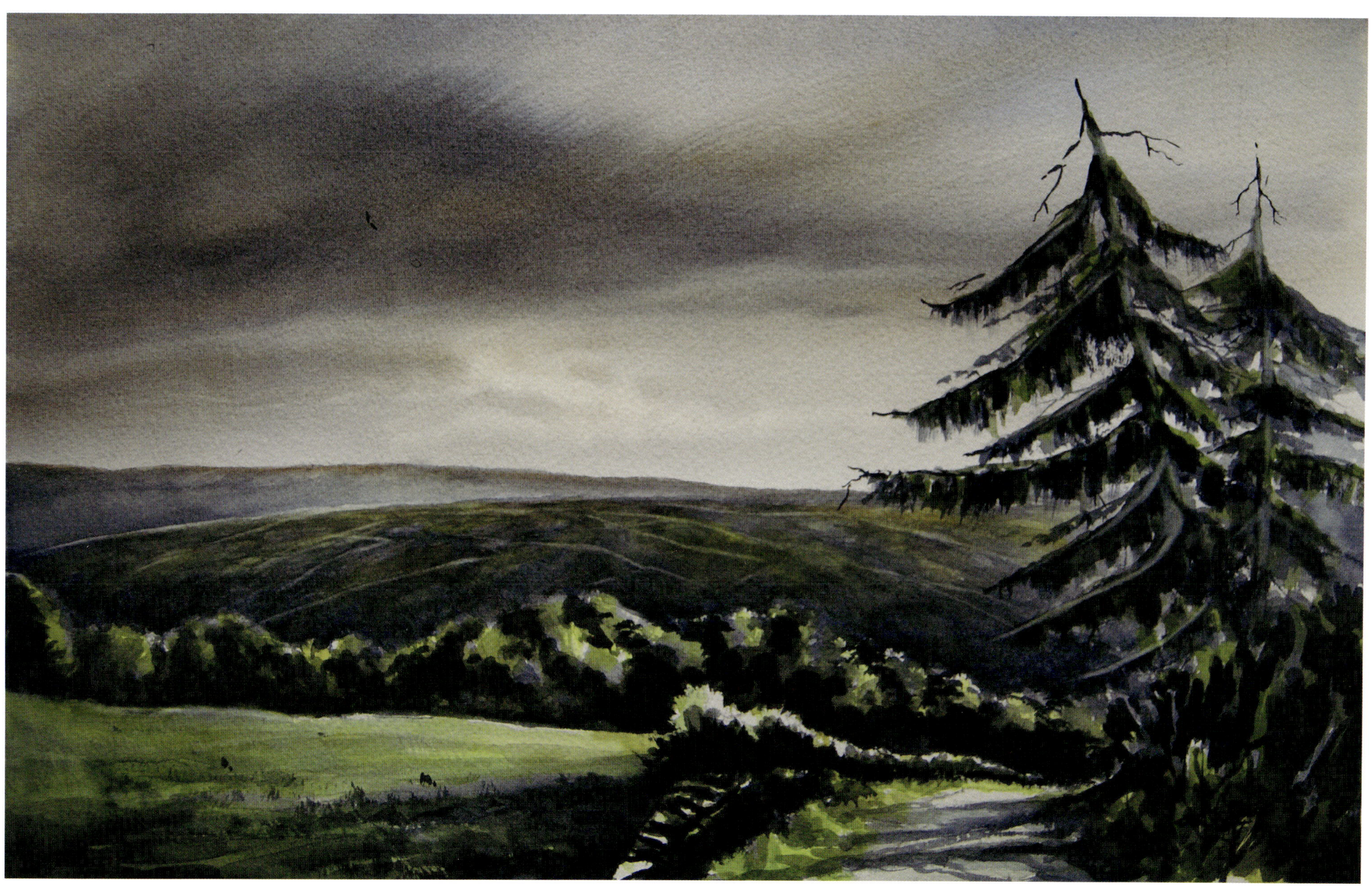

Whitby

Whitby's skyline is dominated by the ruins of St. Hilda's Abbey, high on Whitby's East Cliff. Spilling down below are a maze of alleyways and narrow streets created by the close proximity of the houses clinging to the landscape: they appear to be built on top of one another in the battle for space. From the old town of Whitby, should you be adventurous 199 steps lead up to the parish church of St. Mary, whose churchyard provided the inspirational setting for Bram Stoker's *Dracula*. Many a chip has been stolen by the seagulls on this pier.

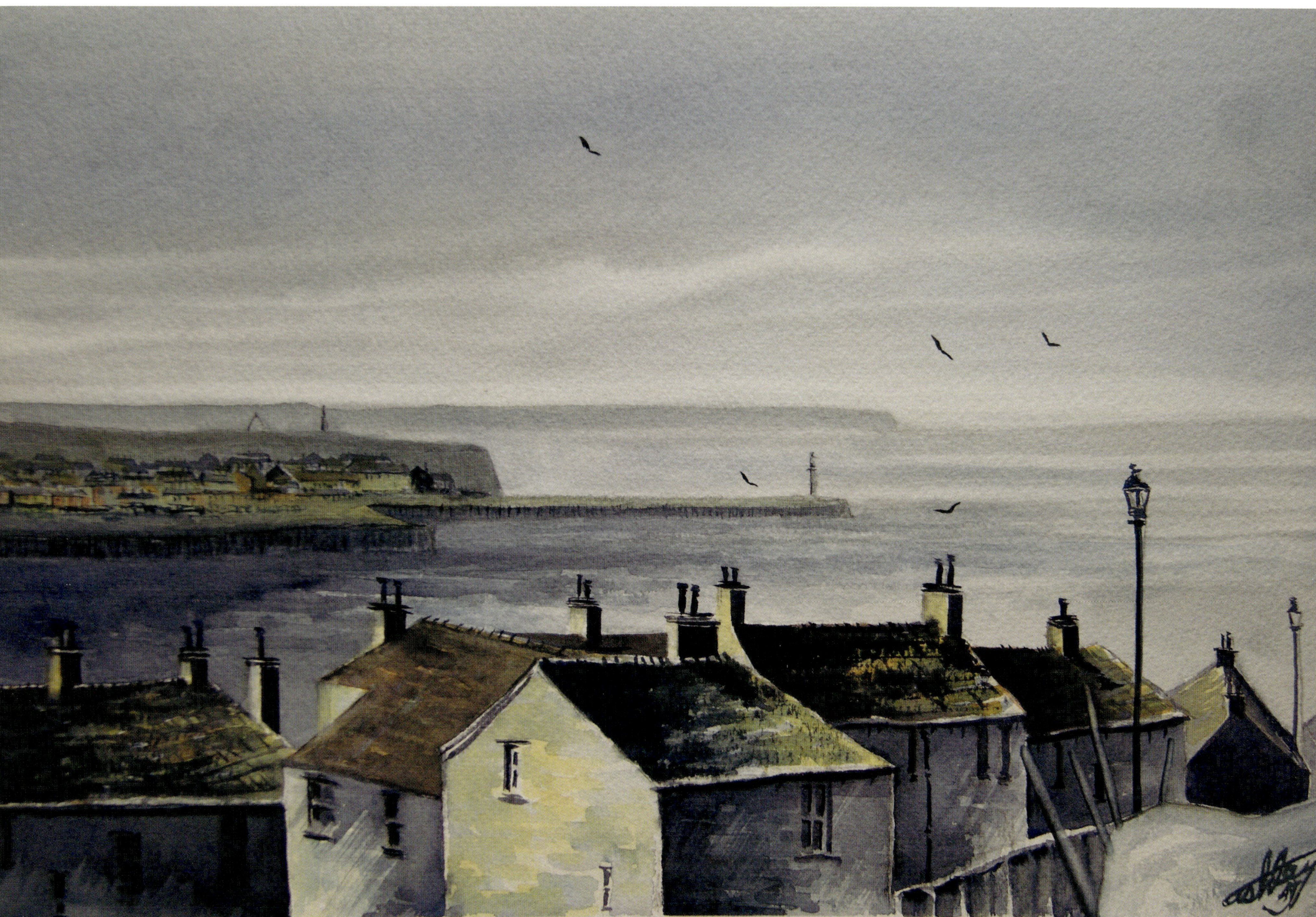

When the Dark Meets the Light on the Landscape

This is the atmosphere that drives me, the rawness of storm so real that you can taste it in the air.

Unlike others, as an artist I feel drawn to the moors on the most inhospitable days, days when other rational people's inbuilt natural desire is to remain safe . . . mine is to capture the magnitude of the storm. To capture this moment you have to feel it, so that there is no escaping that 'wow' feeling that cannot be explained but only felt.

Like a window to heaven the light in the sky is reflected on to the landscape below and whether you believe in God or Mother Nature, this is truly an instance to reflect on man's frailties.

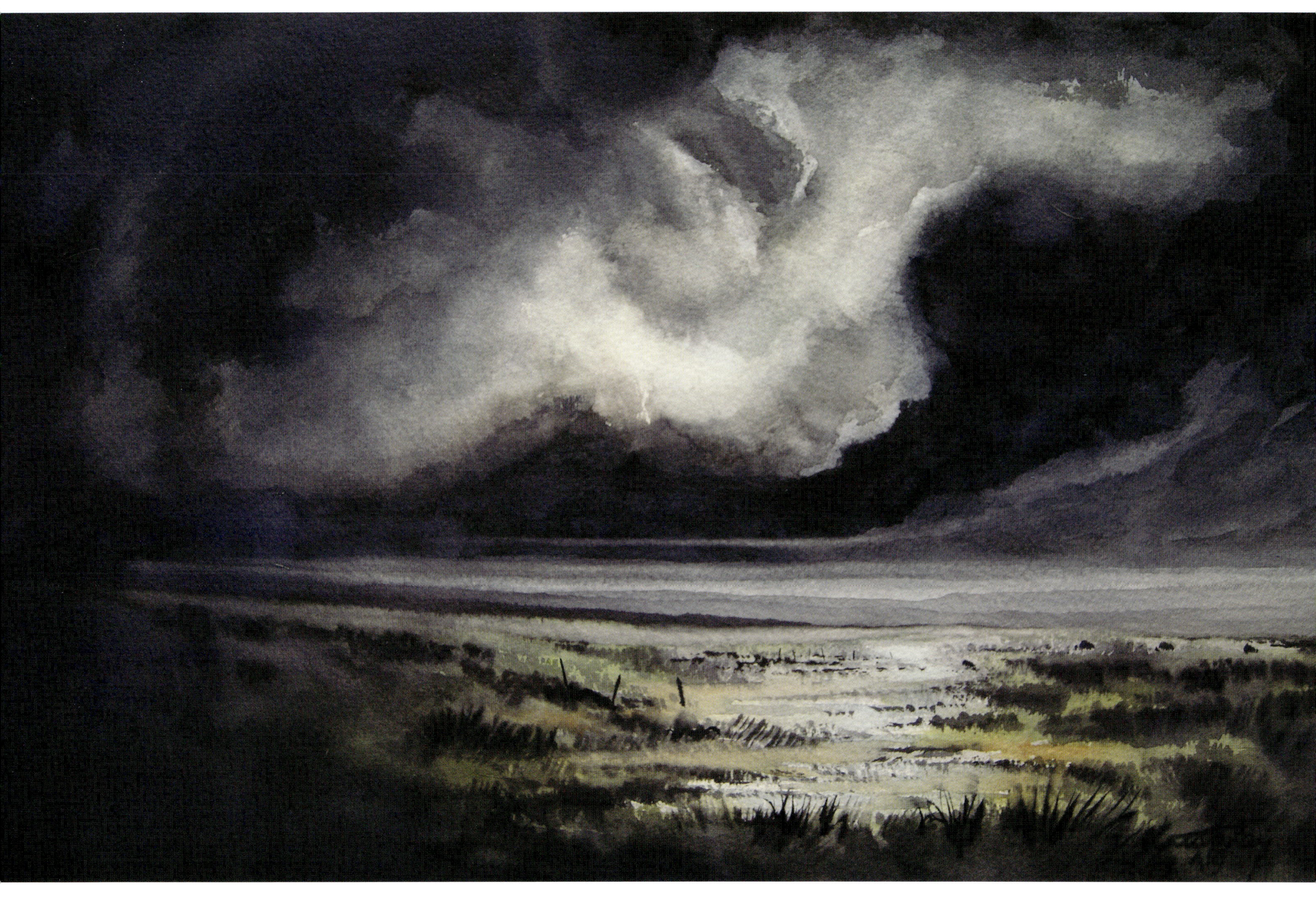

Kilnsey

Kilnsey Crag, the majestic lion's head that overlooks Wharfedale, represents to me the epitome of what a man can achieve when taken to the limits; it encapsulates the strength and magnitude of the county and its people. The lion's head is one of my favourite sculptures of all time, sculptured from stone by Nature herself. I also believe that it is not by chance that the lion, which is the emblem of Great Britain, shows her head so magnificently in the heart of Yorkshire.

The distinctive Kilnsey Crag is a towering inland limestone cliff, around 50 metres high, which has an impressive overhang of about 12 metres created by the Wharfedale glacier during the Ice Age. The British artist that has inspired me, J.M.W. Turner, visited the Crag on his tour of Yorkshire in 1816, deciding to paint from the southern aspect. I have been fortunate with the assistance of Jamie Roberts, Managing Partner – Kilnsey Park, to walk down the river and stand in the exact location that Turner stood to complete his work of the Crag. Today as then, you have to use artistic licence to capture the location, often moving a tree or raising yourself above the landscape in your mind's eye to provide you with an aerial view. An artist can truly compose a painting compared to a photograph that captures only in two dimensions, thus I never ever use a camera: all my paintings are composed from initial sketches or studies.

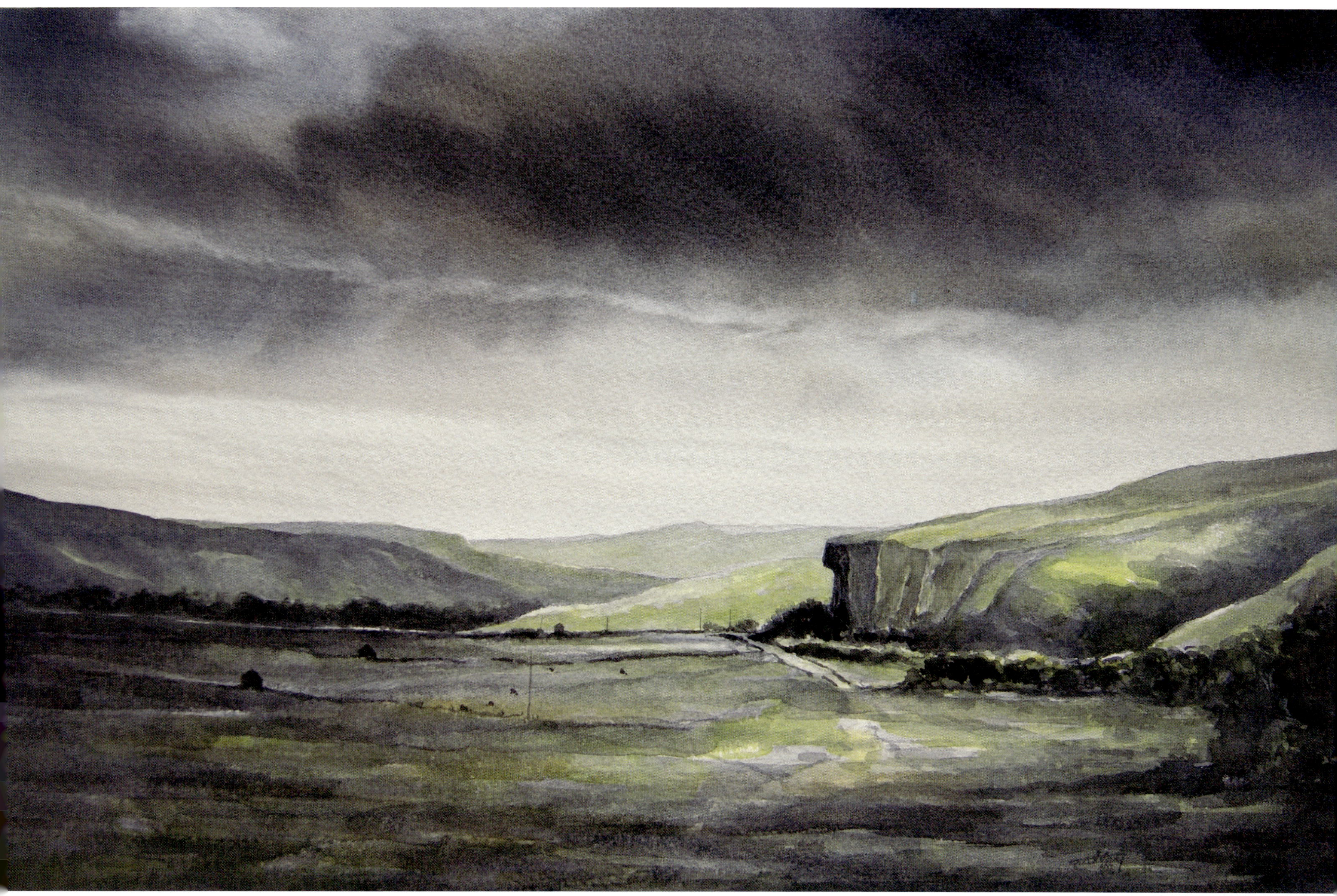

Stoodley Pike from Colne Rd

What a dramatic valley, where the mills and farms meet the moors, the meeting of the textile chain from sheep to mill in one short distance. Look closely and you will see the opening between the drystone walls at the forefront of the painting. This allows your eye to enter the landscape and to keep your interest in the cottages on the left and the monument at Stoodley Pike in the distance.

It might seem a simple thing but if there had been a solid wall or closed gate you would have felt there was something wrong with the painting but you might not have known why . . . it would have acted as a mental barrier.

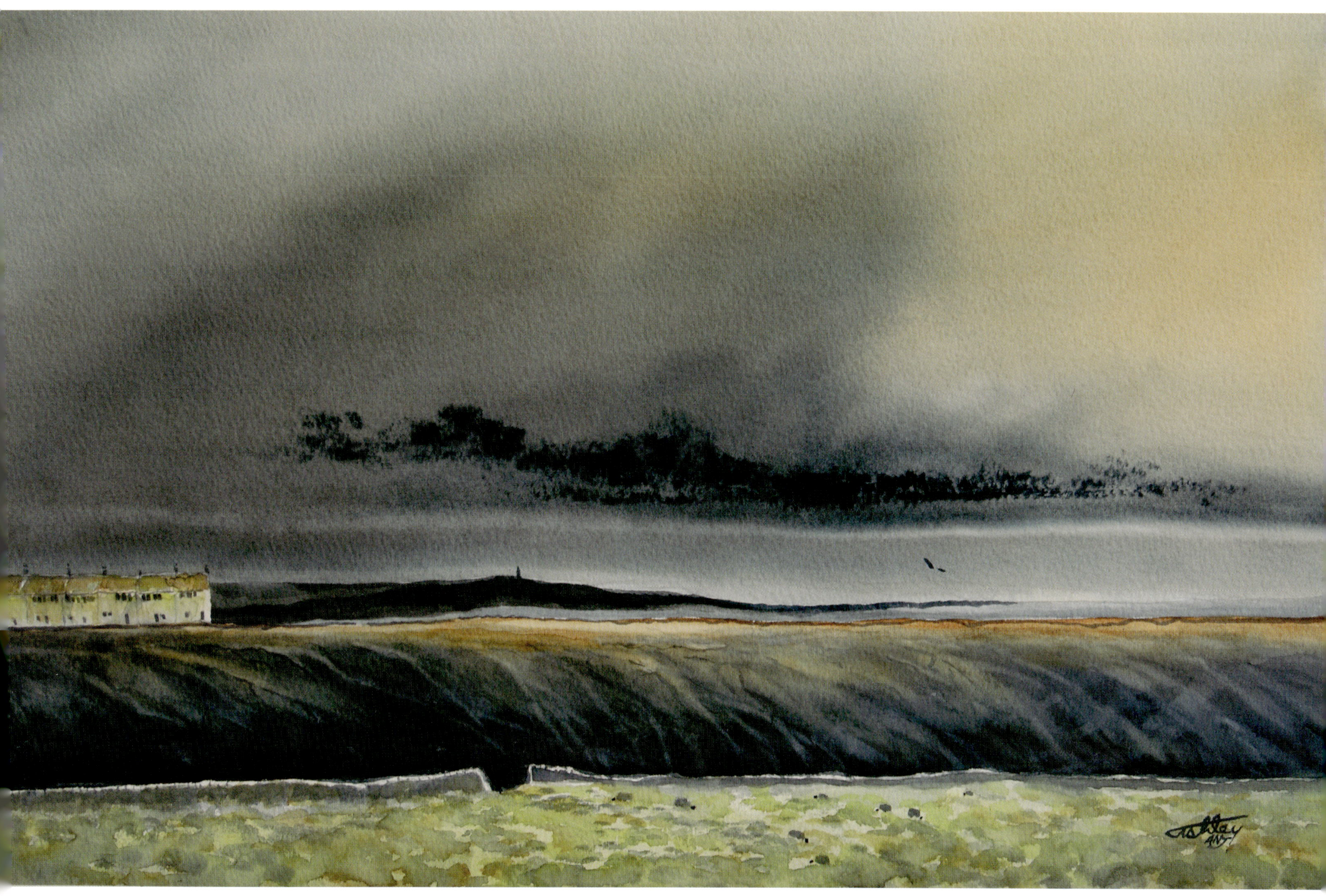

Stoodley Pike from Colne Rd   139

Biography

It has been sixty years since Yorkshire watercolour artist Ashley Jackson joined the art profession. Throughout this time it has been his unwillingness to deviate from his love affair with Yorkshire that has allowed him to intimately capture her every emotion. Without words he views her raw contours through the eyes of a man that has been absorbed in the passion of a 'young man' in a hurry to investigate, to touch, to taste, to utilise every human sense available, to today; older, wiser, more knowledgeable but no less in love with his mistress, the Yorkshire landscape.

He has not only wished to capture the moorland with his own eyes but also been vocally passionate in attempting to lead others to visit Yorkshire and the Dales to see in person all that Mother Nature has to offer. Ashley states, 'You cannot smell the wet heather, hear the skylark as she circles to protect her eggs or feel the atmosphere change as rain approaches from a screen, all of these can only be felt by using our senses out in the great Cathedral of the open air.'

It is this dogmatic persistence that has seen his paintings exhibited in the most unusual settings. Ashley's watercolour *Earth to Earth, Life's Pathway*, was unveiled on a Yorkshire Bank debit card in 2009, it was believed to be the first time art had been reproduced in this way. He said providing art for the debit card met his ambitions to raise the profile of art and Yorkshire. He added: 'People will genuinely have a piece of Yorkshire in their pocket – representing Yorkshire and art wherever they use the card, be it New York, London or Newcastle.' What a fantastic calling card . . .

Encapsulating his philosophy of 'Bringing Art to the People' a train named *Ashley Jackson – The Yorkshire Artist* was launched in 2010: again no one could question his commitment and passion to his mistress, Yorkshire, as reproductions of his paintings were unveiled within the carriages of the exclusively-named Grand Central train. Having exhibited all over the world, Ashley has strived throughout his life to make art accessible to everyone, thus the concept of art being placed within everyday life experiences, without people having to frequent galleries, seemed a natural progression.

At the launch, Ashley explained, 'This is a fantastic day for Art, Yorkshire and the Country as it opens up a new exhibition space that allows us to have artistic experiences

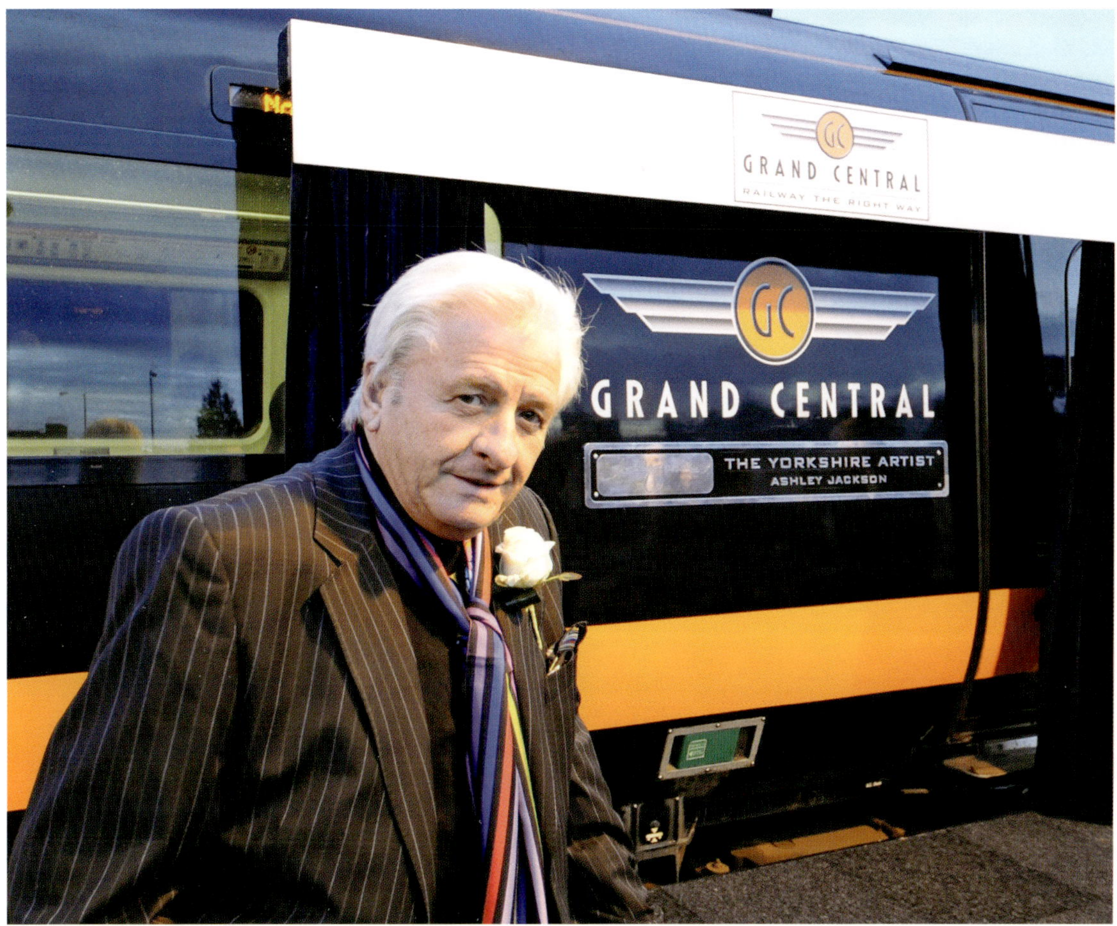

within the confines of our working day, hopefully making train journeys a little more pleasant and thought-provoking. I have always said that Yorkshire is my mistress, painting the landscape as if they were her contours on the most inhospitable days, through these paintings and words from my sketch book I hope that others will begin to share my passion and enthusiasm for God's County – Yorkshire.'

Amongst many awards and accolades Ashley was presented by the University of Huddersfield in 2013 with a Honorary Doctorate(Uni), for his commitment to the Arts, a fantastic accolade to be bestowed by a committee of his peers, for his dedication to a lifetime campaign of making art accessible to all. The University further strengthened their relationship with paintings on display within Student Central, the main focal point of the University, this is also open to the general public to view.

> *His work captures the beauty and identity of Yorkshire in a way that few others have ever achieved and his work is now recognised across the world. Ashley is a fabulously gifted artist and his vision, as he would say 'to bring art to the public', in particular to young people, is to be commended.*
> (Vice-Chancellor of the University of Huddersfield, Professor Bob Cryan)

He has lost none of his momentum in his drive to not only encourage people to take up art, but to appreciate the beauty of the landscape around us. 'Framing the Landscape' is such a project created by Ashley: in an initial sketch of a frame on the landscape the concept was born. 'I want children to see the drama of Mother Nature and how a landscape changes every second,' he says. 'I want them to come away saying, "Wow. I didn't know we had this land". My passion is for a new generation to look at the land – and begin to look after it, education is the paramount and through art I hope to impassion young hearts and minds.'

Alongside Marsden Moor, Brimham Rocks, Roseberry Topping and Hardcastle Crags each frame location highlights the diverse nature of the Yorkshire landscape that surrounds us and perhaps we take for granted. The 6ft free-standing metal frames ensure the focus is firmly placed on what the eye can see through the frame; the rich warmth of the autumn moor, the afternoon sunlight across the valley, the Henry Moore-inspiring balancing rocks of Brimham and how the industrial heritage has blended with the natural landscape. Framing both Castle Hill and Emley Mast, the Holme Moss Frame focuses the eye on many of the landscapes that Ashley has captured in his own paintings.

Ashley would be the first to admit that his life has been shaped by the loss of his father, at the hands of the Japanese in the Second World War, and his mother remarrying a Yorkshireman who brought them both to live in Huddersfield and then Barnsley. It was perhaps this innate melancholy that drew Ashley to the atmospheric drama of the open moorland as he states, 'As an artist I have been privileged to view the moors with an honest clarity, the drama of the sky with an approaching storm, the crispness of fresh fallen snow under foot or the damp chill of drizzling rain. The landscape is more than a passing view from a car window it is our heritage, culture and more personally it forms part of our thoughts and feelings.'

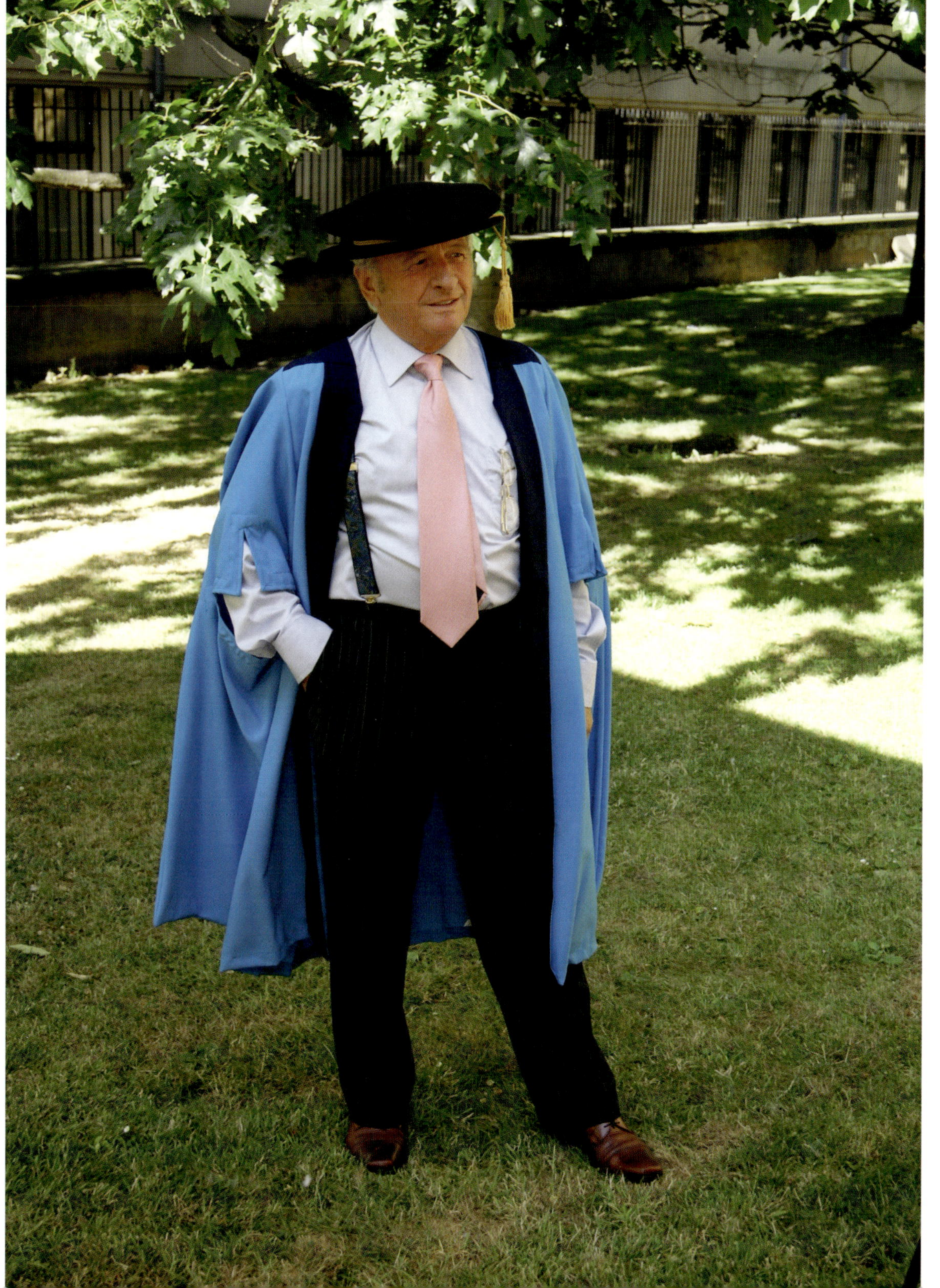

Final Words from Ashley

The last page in the book should be given to the sketch of Ewden Valley, a watercolour sketch, for it was painted from a sketch I undertook on my first date with Anne Hutchinson, the woman I was later to marry and the only woman other than my mistress the moors that has seen me stripped bare emotionally. For it is Anne that has been my foundation and confidence, purchasing this very painting so that it could not be sold to anyone else, standing alongside me from my very first gallery at Dodworth in 1963, through to Barnsley 1968 and then to the gallery opening in Holmfirth in 1986.

We still have the painting hung at home as a reminder of how far this pathway has taken me, my life has been shaped by two factors; the death of my father and the Yorkshire landscape. Unfortunately I could not have had one without the other, which is a cause of great sadness to me.

One must never give up
Although some people would like to see you giving up.
To be a painter is easy
To be an Artist is a great gift.
The painter just paints pictures,
But the Artist puts his soul into his paintings.
So the painter gives you a picture
And the Artist gives the world a painting.
(Ashley Jackson, 1968)

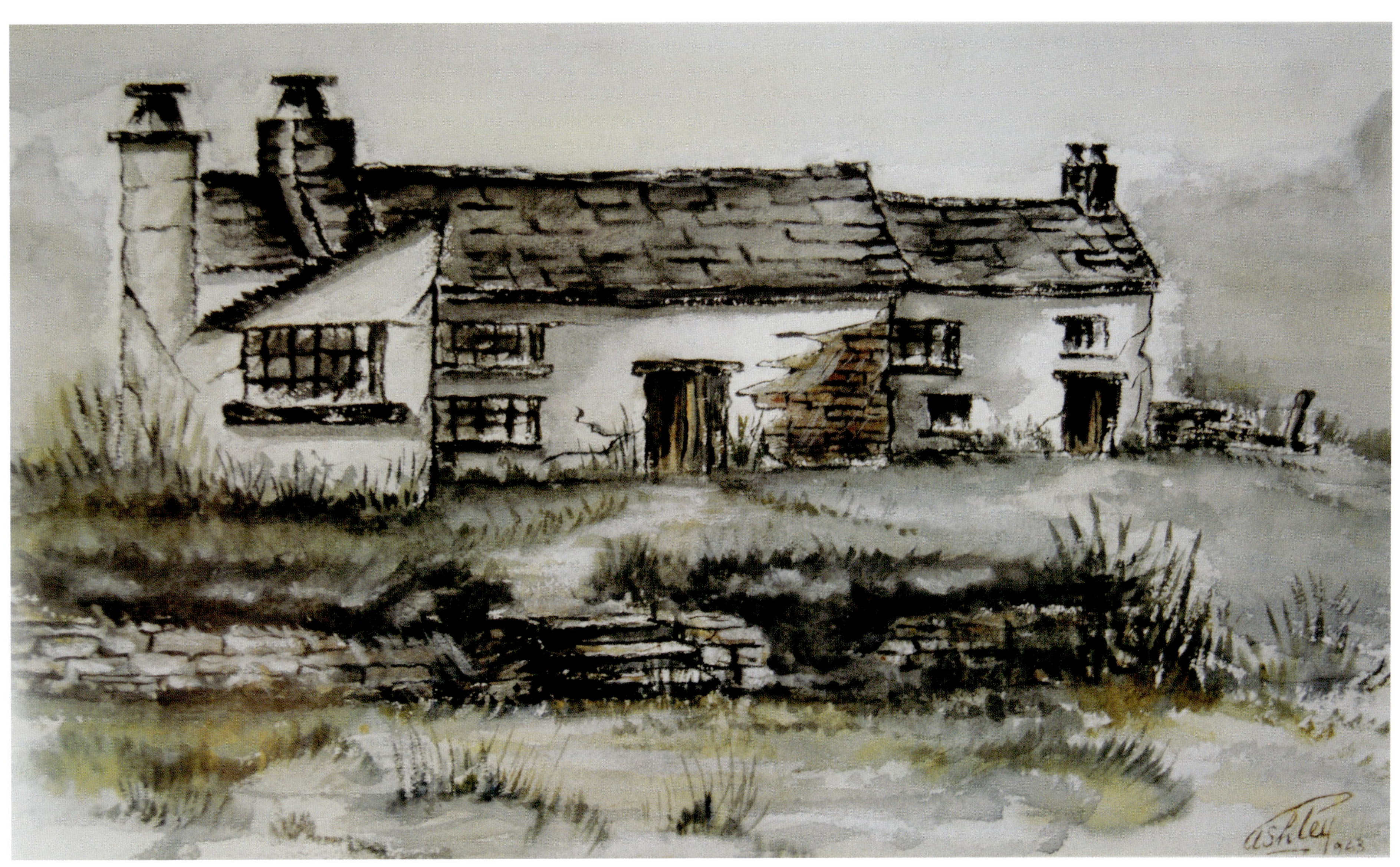

Index of Paintings

Available to View as Prints in the Gallery

Earth to Earth, Life's Pathway – small print. (no longer available)

When All Have Gone Home – small print.

Power and the Passion – differing sizes.

When the Curtain Comes Down – small print.

Moving Light – Gordale Scar – print collection

Solace from the Storm – signed print collection.

The End of the Day – limited-edition print.

The Sun Rises on a New Day – print collection.

Coming Home before the Rain – limited-edition print.

Meltham in the Snow – signed print collection.

The Red Postbox, Yockenthwaite – signed print collection.

The Road Less Travelled – signed print collection.

I Feel the Power – panoramic print collection.

When Winter Moves In – Bolster Moor – panoramic print collection.

Wuthering Heights – signed print collection. (no longer available)

Farm on Blackshaw Moor – print collection.

Foxup – print collection.

All other paintings are held in private collections of which we are grateful for the permission to utilize in this book.

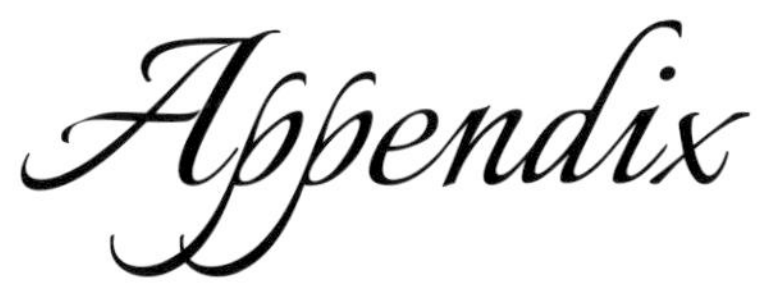

Appendix

One-man Exhibitions

2013 September – January 2014
'Chasing Light', The Biscuit Factory, Newcastle.

2013 5 July – 9 August
'Celebrating God's Own County', Bradford Cathedral.

2010 22 October – 8 May 2011
'Power and the Passion', previously unseen work celebrating his
70th year displayed at Temple Newsam House, Leeds.

2010 4–9 October
'Power and the Passion' previously unseen work celebrating his 70th
year displayed at the prestigious Mall Galleries, London.

2008 26 July – 20 October
'Painting in the open air', previously unseen work displayed
at the prestigious Laing Art Gallery, Newcastle.

2003 13 September – 13 October
'Ashley Jackson One Man Exhibition', at Patchings Art Farm, Calverton Notts.

2003
'Ashley Jackson's Yorkshire' – International Yorkshire Business
Convention Centre, Yorkshire Showground.

2002
'Ashley Jackson's Yorkshire Moors – a love affair', Victoria Quarter, Leeds.

2002
'The Spirit Never Dies', Royal Armouries, Leeds.

2000
‘Dawn’s a New Day’, Royal Armouries, Leeds.

1999
‘Twilight of the Twentieth Century’, Cartwright Hall, Bradford.

1997
‘Earth Wind and Fire’, Salford Art Gallery.

1996
‘From Yorkshire With Love’, touring exhibition, Beningborough Hall, York, Wakefield Art Gallery, Sewerby Hall, Bridlington.

1995
‘Here’s to You, Dad’, touring exhibition, Cooper Art Gallery Barnsley, Smith Gallery Brighouse, Dewsbury Town Hall, Doncaster Art Gallery.

1994
‘My Mistress and I, the Yorkshire Moors’, Rotherham Art Gallery.

1994
Yorkshire Post Headquarters.

1993
Patchings Art Gallery – United Society of Artists.

1992
The Coach House Gallery, Lincoln.

1991
‘In harmony with the Moor’, John Worthy Gallery, Leek.
‘In mood with the Moor’, Lauron Gallery, Ilkley.

1990
‘My Way, – Art to the People’, retrospective exhibition, Huddersfield Art Gallery, sponsored by Yorkshire Television.

1989
St Louis, USA.

1988
New York, USA.

1987
'Ashley Jackson's Vision of Turner in Yorkshire', Bass Headquarters
Huddersfield – opened by H.R.H. The Prince of Wales.

1986
'Ashley Jackson's Vision of Turner', The Mall Galleries.
F.B.A. West End, London. Milan, Italy.

1985
Chicago, USA. New York, USA. Dallas, USA.

1984
Milan, Italy.

1983
The Old Barn, Ruislip.

1982
Washington, USA.

1979
Foyles Gallery, Charing Cross Rd, London. Maclaurin Gallery, Glasgow, Scotland.

1978
Kidderminster Art Gallery.

1977
Municipal Gallery, Valencia Spain.

1974
The Mall Gallery, F.B.A. London.

1969
Upper Grosvenor Gallery, West End, London.

1968
Cannon Hall Gallery, Barnsley. Wakefield Art Gallery.

1967
Brighouse Art Gallery.

1966
Crows Nest Gallery, Dewsbury.

1964
Newark Art Gallery, Nottingham.

1963
Brighouse.

Television Productions

2002
'In a Different Light' – YTV.

2001
Ninth series of 'A Brush With Ashley' – YTV/ New
series filming in the Mediterranean.

2000
Eighth series of 'A Brush With Ashley'.
Half-hour documentary 'Some Days are Diamond', YTV – A celebratory
programme in recognition of Ashley's 60th birthday and contribution to the arts.

1999
Seventh YTV series of 'A Brush With Ashley'.
'*QE2* B'aht at' – six-part series by YTV featuring Ashley aboard the *QE2*.

1998
Sixth YTV series of 'A Brush With Ashley'.

1996
Fifth YTV series of 'A Brush With Ashley'.

1995
Fourth YTV series of 'A Brush With Ashley'.

1994
Wire TV mini-series.

1993
Third YTV, Border and Tyne Tees Television series of 'A Brush With Ashley'.

1992
Second YTV, Border and Tyne Tees Television series of 'A Brush With Ashley'.

1990
'A Brush With Ashley', Yorkshire, Border & Tyne Tees & Television.
1990 BBC Look North, 'Profile of an Artist'.

1990 – 1998
Satellite TV The Learning Channel – 'A Brush With Ashley'.

1984 –1988
'Ashley Jackson's world of Art' – series on P.B.S.

1982
'Making the Most of . . .' Channel 4.

1981
'Once in a Lifetime – My Own Flesh and Blood',
documentary on Ashley, Network TV.

1978 & 1985
Own series on *Pebble Mill at One*.

1968
Omnibus programme, BBC.

Books Published

2012
My Yorkshire Sketchbook – Dalesman.

2010
An Artist's Life – biography written by Chris Bond, Pen and Sword.

2006
50 Golden Years – Dalesman.

2000
Ashley Jackson's Yorkshire Moors – A Love Affair – Dalesman.

1994
Painting the British Isles – a watercolourist's journey – Boxtree.

1993
A Brush With Ashley – Boxtree.

1992
Painting in the Open Air – Harper Collins.

1981
My Brush With Fortune – Secker and Warburg.
Ashley Jackson's Worlds of Art – vols 1, 2 & 3, Alexander Art Corporation
An Artist's Notebook, Luddites.

Accolades

2013
Proud to accept Honorary Doctorate from the University of Huddersfield.

2011
Grand Central name a train *Ashley Jackson – The Yorkshire Artist*.

2009
Yorkshire Bank launch debit card with Ashley Jackson painting.
Yorkshireman of the year, Dalesman Rural Award.

2008
Yorkshire Icon Award and Hall of Fame.

2007
Lifetime Achievement Award – *Huddersfield Examiner*.

2006
Lifetime Achievement Award – Yorkshire Awards.

2005
Freedom of the City of London.

2004 – 2009
Ambassador Northernart.

2004
BT selected one of Ashley's paintings to be depicted on
the front cover of the telephone directory.

1996
Arts and Entertainment Award – Yorkshire Awards.
Yorkshire Society – Vice-Chairman, Vice-President.

1967
Elected Fellow of the Royal Society of Arts.
Founder Member of the Yorkshire Watercolour Society; elected Chairman.

Books
Entry in *Who's Who in Art*, Debretts' Distinguished People of Today.

Photograph Credits

Denis Thorpe: Pages 11, 94

Claudia Berettoni: Pages 38-9, 92, 112, 120, 128, 143

Unknown: Page 141